Is the Voice in My Head God or Just Me?

AN 8-LESSON BIBLE STUDY ON HEARING THE VOICE OF GOD

SANDY COOPER

Copyright © 2020 by Sandy Cooper

Cover Design and interior formatting by Nelly Murariu at PixBeeDesign.com
Author Photo: Green Apple Photography

ISBN: 979-8667688976
Independently Published

Dedication

To Jon,
All because you wanted
to move to Florida...

Contents

For a free Bible Study Leader Guide go to https://thescooponbalance.com/leaderguide/

Introduction

"We may mistakenly think that if God spoke to us, we would automatically know who is speaking, without having to learn, but that is simply a mistake—and one of the most harmful mistakes for those trying to hear God's voice. It leaves us totally at the mercy of any stray ideas we have picked up about what God's speaking is like."

DALLAS WILLARD[1]

I didn't always recognize God's voice.

In fact, for the first 18 years of my life, I wasn't even aware God spoke at all. My parents raised me in a faith tradition where "hearing God's voice" was neither mentioned, nor encouraged. Also, as a young girl, my primary interests did not include Jesus or the Bible, but rather boys and cheerleading. In that order.

Then, in the summer between high school and college, I made a definitive and dramatic confession of faith, forever changing the trajectory of my life. Instantly, God realigned my priorities: *Jesus*, boys, and cheerleading. In that order. For the first time, God awakened me to the reality that He desires to have both a relationship and an on-going conversation with me.

However, for the first 10 years of my walk with Him, I relied almost exclusively on other people—church leaders, mostly—to hear God's voice on my behalf and interpret for me what they heard. As you can imagine, this approach was wrought with issues:

Issue One: I developed zero-desire and zero-ability to seek God for direction on my own. The church leaders were skilled at hearing God's voice, so I was content with them doing so. Before I made a decision, big or small, I first ran it past one of these church leaders and asked them (to ask God and then tell me) what I should do.

Issue Two: I never challenged their interpretation of God's voice to me. They were older, wiser, and far godlier than me. They understood the Bible better than I did. They actually quoted entire Bible passages when they counseled me! For years, I failed to search God's word myself to see whether their interpretations were accurate or their quoted passages were used in context. I assumed their opinion was also God's opinion, always.

Issue Three: Sometimes these people did not agree *with one another.* In a church culture where "God told me" was thrown around like rice on newlyweds, the fact that they "heard" contradictory things should have been a red flag. Instead, I became confused and frustrated while doing my best to keep everyone happy with me. That was, until one night when I could no longer ignore the glaring contradictions.

I stood in the back of my church between two men I loved and admired— my pastor of 10 years and my husband of two years. Jon and I were a young couple seeking our pastor's blessing over the biggest decision we would ever make up to that point—a job change requiring relocation across the country.

Jon—a young, talented executive with a promising future—felt he had clearly heard from God on our behalf regarding this move. So that night, while I stood by his side, he informed our pastor we'd soon be leaving and asked for his blessing.

To our shock, our pastor refused to bless our decision. He, too, felt he had clearly heard from God on our behalf regarding this job. Except, he heard the opposite. He believed moving would be a mistake for us spiritually. He advised us to stay put—in our hometown, in our home church.

My strong-minded husband would not accept this answer about his family, his career, and his future without some pushback. For the next several minutes, I listened to my pastor and my husband discuss, politely yet emphatically, why moving was/was not God's will for our lives.

To be clear, the opportunity was not sinful, dangerous, or sketchy. My pastor had no apparent reason to withhold a blessing from us. The position was in Jon's desired career field, included a pay increase and room for advancement, and was in a beautiful city on the ocean. Plus, my employer advised me I could also apply for a job transfer, meaning I would have work waiting for me there, as well. On paper, everything looked great.

I, however, had my own set of reservations about moving. I wanted to be excited about this move and support Jon in his career, but I was struggling. Moving away meant I would leave everything I had known my entire life—friends, family, and church. All six of my siblings, their families, and my parents lived within five miles of me. I loved the idea of raising my future children near grandparents, aunts, uncles, and cousins. Additionally, my mom's health had been steadily declining for years. Moving 1,000 miles away to a city where we knew no one not only meant I'd lose my entire support system, but also meant I couldn't be home in a moment's notice should an emergency arise with my mom.

To complicate things further, our two-year-old marriage was hanging by a thread. In our short, married life, Jon and I had developed significant communication and trust issues. When we weren't busy fighting our way up the corporate ladder in our respective careers, we were fighting with each other in the privacy of our home. No one knew it, but we fought all the time. Moving away to a strange city sounded lonely and scary to me. I wasn't sure our marriage would survive either way, but at least if we stayed, I had the security of life-long friends and family to support me.

Before that night, Jon and I had spent weeks hashing through the pros and cons of moving. After reaching an impasse, I gave in, but with a giant stipulation: I would agree to move—*but only with our pastor's blessing.* A blessing that, in my immature spiritual mind, would guarantee God's hand on me and on our fragile marriage.

So, picture the three of us standing in the back of our church:

- My husband—the man with whom I was bound by marital covenant, but didn't fully trust—telling me we needed to move;

- My pastor—the man who had guided me through all major life decisions since I was a teen—withholding a blessing (that felt to me like *God* withholding *His* blessing);

- And me—the girl who had been relying on other people to tell her what to do her entire life—standing between them in complete confusion.

Also, picture both my hair and the white collar of my Laura Ashley tea-length floral dress as being massive, because this entire dramatic scene took place in the back of a church in 1996.

In one life-altering moment, as I stood between these two men who loved me and who were trying to decide my future, I heard myself utter the words: **"If I cannot hear the voice of God for myself, what hope do I have?"**

That night, I decided that learning to discern God's voice would become my life-long pursuit. No longer would I depend on other people—neither my pastor nor my husband—to hear from God on my behalf. If God truly spoke to His children, then He could speak to me, too.

I had no idea at the time how that single decision would shape the next two decades. I had no idea that learning to hear the voice of God would be one of the most exciting and liberating experiences of my life. I had no idea how God would open up my understanding of the scriptures on this subject and allow me to experience—for myself— the voice of God as I continued to walk with Him.

✿

This Bible study is the result of that pursuit. This is everything I've learned thus far about hearing and following God's voice. It's not the final word on hearing God—not by a long shot. Many authors and Bible scholars more talented than me have written on this subject, and I will reference some of them throughout this book. I encourage you to read them in addition to this.

✿

My personal study and pursuit to know God and His voice has been messy and difficult. Turns out, this topic is controversial. I've learned the hard way that Christians can get ugly when you challenge their doctrine. I've heard Christians condemn other Christians to eternal damnation over divisive interpretation of Scripture, sometimes stemming from only one passage taken out of context. I've seen abhorrent social media accounts created to discredit and defame well-known Bible teachers who claim to hear God's voice. I've heard "prophets" spew out foolishness, and I've listened to humble servants of God utter prophecy, to their own surprise and delight.

I've pored over hundreds of books, Bible studies, articles, Bible commentaries, and podcasts, seeking clarification on God, the Church, the Bible, and God's voice.

Along the way, I adopted, fought for, pledged to die for, and later discarded the *exact same doctrinal beliefs*.

At one point, I was so confused by conflicting opinions from all sides that I sat down in the middle of my living room floor with my Bible open to God and cried, "All I know for sure is You are God, and the Bible is Your word. Beyond that, it's all fair game. I pledge to know nothing. I'm starting over. Lead me into Truth."

Like I said: messy.

So, lean in, dear reader, and listen carefully when I tell you this:

After all I've seen, heard, and learned, I've never been more convinced that God speaks. Make no mistake, the God of the Bible spoke whenever He wanted, to whomever He wanted, however He wanted—*and people heard Him when He did.*

Psalm 29

A psalm of David.
Ascribe to the Lord, you heavenly beings,
ascribe to the Lord glory and strength.

Ascribe to the Lord the glory due his name;
worship the Lord in the splendor of his holiness.

The voice of the Lord is over the waters;
the God of glory thunders,
the Lord thunders over the mighty waters.

The voice of the Lord is powerful;
the voice of the Lord is majestic.
The voice of the Lord breaks the cedars;
the Lord breaks in pieces the cedars of Lebanon.
He makes Lebanon leap like a calf,
Sirion like a young wild ox.

The voice of the Lord strikes
with flashes of lightning.

The voice of the Lord shakes the desert;
the Lord shakes the Desert of Kadesh.

The voice of the Lord twists the oaks
and strips the forests bare.
And in his temple all cry, "Glory!"

The Lord sits enthroned over the flood;
the Lord is enthroned as King forever.
The Lord gives strength to his people;
the Lord blesses his people with peace.

(Emphasis mine.)

The God of the Bible is the God of today. He has not changed. He wants us to know Him and to know His will. He does not take pleasure in our confusion. He is not playing games or trying to keep us in the dark. He speaks, and we *will* know when He does.

Jesus said, *"I no longer call you servants, because a servant does not know his master's business. Instead, I have called you friends, for everything that I learned from my Father I have made known to you." John 15:15*

If the concept of hearing God's voice is new or strange to you, I ask you to keep an open heart and mind as you work through this study. Hold everything—the content of this book as well as your personally held beliefs—up to God's Word. Don't be afraid to wrestle with doctrines and assertions. I have found that wrestling with beliefs, doctrines, and assertions promotes spiritual health and resilience. Wrestling is an incredible act of intimacy. I think God welcomes it when we approach Him with pure motives and a humble heart.

As you wrestle, if you encounter something that does not align with God's Word, discard it. God's Word was and is *always* the final authority.

By the way, as a Christian, I believe the entire Bible, (the Old and New Testaments combined) comprise the Holy Scriptures—the very words of God. I believe the Bible to be absolutely true and authoritative, and without error or contradiction. Unfortunately, I don't have space in this Bible study to examine all the reasons why Christians trust the Scriptures to be the word of God. So, if you have doubts, I encourage you to set this Bible study aside and first examine this issue of the authority of Scripture on your own. Seriously, this entire study is built on the premise that the Bible is God's word, so you will get very little out of this study if you don't first establish this premise in your own heart and mind.

❀

WHAT YOU WILL NEED

- A Bible. I use NIV unless otherwise noted, so you will need access to an NIV for the fill-in-the blanks. Please be aware that the NIV was updated in 2011, so your version may differ slightly even if you are also using NIV. If you do not own an NIV, you can easily access it for free on line at Biblegateway.com. Other than that, you can use whatever translation you prefer for most of the study.

- A pen to write your answers

- Colored pens, pencils, and a highlighter, if that's your jam

- A journal, if you want to write more than space allows

WHAT TO EXPECT (AND WHAT NOT TO EXPECT)

This is a topical study as opposed to a line-by-line study. Henry Blackaby in his book, *Hearing God's Voice*, points out that, *"The Bible is a collection of accounts that reveal God speaking to people to give them specific instructions they would never have known otherwise. No matter where you look, you will find God's specific instructions to his people.*[2]*"* In other words, in order to do a line-by-line study on hearing God's voice, we'd need to literally study the entire Bible, line-by-line. As you can imagine, that would take a while.

So, while this is a topical study, I do my best to "rightly divide" the word of God. By that I mean I approach the Scriptures in the context and genre with which they were intended. Therefore, while it is time-consuming, I will periodically ask you to read an entire chapter before we discuss a shorter passage within it. I will also offer any relevant cultural or contextual information you will need to understand the passage. Then, I will ask questions that will require you to dig out answers from both the text and related passages. This simple process will teach you to study God's word on your own and avoid theological errors.

I try to give you plenty of creative ways to interact with the passages we study. The word of God is alive and active. And, call me a nerd if you want, but I think studying God's word is fun. I want your Bible study time to be your favorite time of the day.

Here is a brief overview of what you will see throughout the lessons:

- **Summary:** This is a way for you to restate the main points of what you just learned. Sometimes I will provide this for you and sometimes I'll ask you to do it. Periodically summarizing what you are learning helps you to retain the information.

- **Write the verse/fill in the blank:** When I want to emphasize a passage, I will ask you to write it word-for-word or fill in the blanks. This is not just busy-work. I have found in my own study of God's word that writing out a passage with my own hand is an effective way of slowing down and absorbing the words into my heart and mind.

- **Apply:** Here I will ask you to take what you just learned and integrate it into your life. This Bible study is meant to instruct you so that you can change. The application process is vital to growth.

- **Reflect and Assess:** In these sections, I will ask you to think about your own life, maybe recall a personal example or consider where you are right now in your thinking or your habits. It's important to identify your current position so you can track growth over time.

- **Pause and listen:** This is one of the most meaningful sections of the whole study. My prayer is that you not only learn *about* hearing God's voice, but also learn *to* hear God's voice.

- **Dig Deeper:** If you have more time and want to study a topic in greater depth than what I've written, I will sometimes offer additional direction to accomplish that.

- **For Discussion:** If you are studying this with a group, I've listed a few suggested questions at the end of each lesson that can guide your group discussion. (If you are leading a group and would like to download a free Leader's Guide, go to https://thescooponbalance.com/leaderguide/). If you are studying alone, you can use these questions for personal reflection or journaling prompts. I will always conclude each lesson with the question, "What is your biggest takeaway?" This is one of my favorite questions to ask myself in my own personal study. It will help you pinpoint what you are learning as you go and it creates an easy way to reference the material in the study that was most relevant to you.

Here's one final tip: Take as much time as you need with each lesson. I purposely did not break the lessons up into "days" or imply that each lesson should take "a week" to complete. Your spiritual enemy oppresses you with enough stress and pressure in every other area of your life— I don't want your time in God's word to be one of them. If you have an hour a day to study, perfect. If you have five minutes every other day, also perfect. If you want to linger over a lesson for weeks, I encourage this. And if you find yourself following a trail of related scriptures off this study entirely, by all means, go there! This is where the good stuff happens. In short, your pace is the correct pace, and God will lead you where He wants you to go. As a general point of reference, early readers of this study tracked the length of time it took them to complete each lesson. Their times varied anywhere from one hour to three hours per lesson. You'll notice, for example, that Lesson One is significantly shorter than the others. So don't assume that each lesson will take the same amount of time.

❀

After that pivotal moment in the back of my church over 20 years ago, I decided to honor my covenant with Jon, cling to my fragile marriage, and move with him to that new city. Sadly, we left without our pastor's blessing, which was devastating to me at the time. But God proved to us that His blessing supersedes any human blessing, given or withheld.

That move turned out to be one of the best decisions we had ever made as a couple, hands down. God faithfully guided us through the uncertainty and fear, and miraculously restored our marriage. Jon and I fell in love with that new city, our new church, and our new neighbors. More importantly, we fell in love with each other. I was right, moving to a place where we knew no one *was* scary, but it provided a perfect opportunity for us to get to know each other. I discovered that I really liked Jon—still do, actually. As I write this book, we are preparing to celebrate our 27th wedding anniversary.

When we received another opportunity just eight years later to relocate again, I bawled like a baby. I didn't want to leave. However, this time, I didn't cry for fear of missing God's voice, His blessing, or His will for my life. No. I cried because I hated saying goodbye to the people whom I'd grown to love like family and to the city that felt like home. This time we were sad, but also excited. This time, Jon and I sought God *together* and moved on to the next adventure *unified*. This move we made with confidence that God was indeed leading us, because we were hearing His voice.

"Whether you turn to the right or to the left,
your ears will hear a voice behind you, saying,
'This is the way; walk in it.'"

ISAIAH 30:21

Lesson One

Created to Hear God
THE SHEPHERD/SHEEP RELATIONSHIP

"The one who enters by the gate is the shepherd of the sheep. The gatekeeper opens the gate for him, and the sheep listen to his voice. He calls his own sheep by name and leads them out. When he has brought out all his own, he goes on ahead of them, and his sheep follow him because they know his voice. But they will never follow a stranger; in fact, they will run away from him because they do not recognize a stranger's voice."

JOHN 10:2-5

A baby knows the voice of her momma. While the entire birthing experience is one massive, mind-blowing miracle after another, one of my favorite memories is the first time my newborn, at the ripe old age of ten seconds, turned toward the sound of my voice.

I was strapped to a table for a cesarean section waiting to be stitched up, when the doctor brought this tiny human up to my face for a brief introduction. With doctors and nurses buzzing around the noisy room, I called my baby by her name for the very first time.

"Well, hello there, Rebekah."

Her neck strained to turn her head toward me, and our eyes locked. No one needed to tell her who I was. After 38 weeks in my womb, she emerged with all the tiny body parts as well as the physical ability necessary to recognize my voice over the others.

This was not the case with my adopted daughter, though. She spent 40 weeks in the womb of her biological mother. Then she spent the next 13 months in the home of her foster mother. Though Elliana had fully functioning ears to recognize familiar voices, none of those voices was mine.

When I met her for the first time in the lobby of a Guatemalan hotel, I came prepared to win her affections with a baby doll and a soft lavender blankie. I played peek-a-boo. I used my best sing-songy voice. I moved all around the room, trying to remain in her line of vision. And when I held out my hands to her so I could hold her in my arms, she turned the other way. She clung tightly to her foster mother and buried her face into the woman's chest. She didn't know me. She didn't know my voice. I was a stranger to her.

✤

God created you with the ability to hear Him.

The same way you have physical eyes to see light and color, nerve-endings to feel temperature and texture, and physical ears to hear tones and volume, you have spiritual ears to hear the voice of God.

If ever a flagship Bible passage on hearing God's voice exists, it is **John 10**. It's a perfect place to begin.

In your Bible, **read John 10:1-21**, and we'll dissect it, verse-by-verse.

THE AUDIENCE

To whom was Jesus speaking?[5] (v. 1, v. 6, and v. 19)

_____

What was their first response after hearing what Jesus said? (v. 6)

_____

After Jesus attempted to clarify and go into greater detail, the listeners had two distinct opinions about Jesus and His words. Summarize the two responses: (vv. 19-21)

_____

_____

_____

_____

Jesus' words often sparked controversy, and this was no exception. Paying particular attention to verses 1, 5, and 8, why do you think these words upset the Pharisees?

_____

_____

_____

_____

THE METAPHOR

If you live in the Western Hemisphere in the 21st century, a metaphor about sheep herding could be unfamiliar and hard to identify with. I personally have never met a shepherd. I have only seen live sheep a few times, at a petting zoo on a school field trip. Even if I wanted to see a shepherd and his sheep in action, I have no idea where the nearest sheep pen is in relation to my home. (I just asked Siri to show me "sheep pens near me," and she responded, "I could not find any matching writing instrument suppliers near you." Even Siri is confused.)

Jesus was not trying to confuse His audience. Instead, He was drawing an analogy from one of the most common practices in the ancient Near East during the first century. His Jewish audience understood every nuance of the metaphor.

It would be as clear to them as if I were speaking to you about driving a car, or picking up milk and eggs at the grocery store, or texting on your smartphone. I wouldn't need to do much explaining. You'd immediately understand the details of these practices because you probably do them every day. So, for us to fully understand what Jesus was saying in this passage of Scripture, we'll need to learn a little bit about sheep herding in the first century.

Read John 10:1-4

Jesus began by talking about the sheep pen (v.1). A sheep pen frequently held several flocks; and when the time came to go out in the morning pasture, each shepherd separated his sheep from the others by his *peculiar call* (v.3).

Western shepherds usually drive their sheep, often using a sheepdog. Their Near Eastern counterparts, on the other hand, both now and in Jesus' day, led their flocks by beckoning them on *with their voice.* Wherever they went, the shepherd preceded them, guiding them to adequate pasture and guarding against possible danger (v.4).

Fill in the blanks for **John 10:4** (Remember, I'm using NIV, so if you have a different version, just write the verse out below instead):

"When he has brought out _____ ,
he goes on ahead of them, and his sheep _____
_____ because they _____ ."

REFLECT AND ASSESS

Jesus was very plain here. He will call His people, and they will know His voice. As you begin this study, how confident do you feel about knowing and recognizing God's voice today?

Not confident at all   **Extremely confident**

① ② ③ ④ ⑤ ⑥ ⑦ ⑧ ⑨ ⑩

Why did you choose that number?

_____

_____

_____

_____

_____

Read John 10:5

The sheep refused to follow a stranger because his voice was unfamiliar. In fact, if a stranger should use the shepherd's call and imitate his tone, the flock would instantly detect the difference and would scatter in panic. (In Lesson Seven, we will learn about the other voices, and how to distinguish the difference between them and the voice of the Shepherd.)

REFLECT AND ASSESS

Think about the "voice of a stranger." What are some of the strange voices you hear? What voices are you tempted to follow? What do they say to you? For example, I often hear a voice that says, "Everyone knows this except for you."

_____

_____

_____

_____

_____

_____

_____

_____

How do these other voices make you feel? In my example, the voice makes me feel inadequate and dumb. Take a moment to reflect on the words you hear inside your brain, using as much detail as possible.

_____

_____

_____

_____

_____

_____

_____

_____

Skip past verses 6-10 and read verses 11-15 (we'll come back to verses 6-10 later).

Usually, when I hear someone reference this passage, they say that Jesus likened us to sheep because sheep are, well..._stupid_. Maybe I'm a big baby, but I bristle when I think of God calling me "stupid." This doesn't sound like something a loving Father would say to His daughter, neither does it seem consistent with the tone or point of this passage.

To be sure, sheep are single-minded, skittish, and near-sighted. They are one of the few animals that, if left on their own, would destroy their pasture. They are easily terrified and prone to wander off from the flock. They require constant attention. They will repeatedly wander and get into dangerous situations without learning to avoid them. Yes, yes...all of that is true, of sheep _and of me_.

But I don't believe Jesus chose to compare us to sheep because of their stupidity. I think He called us sheep because of their _tremendous value_.

Sheep in Jesus' day were a vital part of life. They were used for food and for clothing. They provided a livelihood for people. A good shepherd did not envision his responsibility as just a keeper of stupid sheep. The care and protection of the flock was the shepherd's whole life.

The Prophet Ezekiel uses this metaphor extensively, explaining the many ways the Shepherd cares for His sheep. **Read the entire chapter of Ezekiel 34, and then complete all the "I will" statements found in verses 11-16.** I filled out the first one for you (some verses have more than one).

V. 11: I will *search for my sheep and look after them*

V. 12: I will _____

V. 12: I will _____

V. 13: I will _____

V. 13: I will _____

V. 13: I will _____

V. 14: I will _____

V. 15: I will _____

V. 16: I will _____

V. 16: I will _____

V. 16: I will _____

V. 16: I will _____

Write Ezekiel 34:31 word-for-word:

_____

_____

_____

Now flip back to **John 10** and reread verses 12 and 13, taking note of how Jesus differentiates between the shepherd and the hired hand and fill in the blanks below:

"The _____ is not the shepherd and does not _____ the sheep. So when he sees the wolf coming, he _____ the sheep and _____ . Then the wolf attacks the flock and scatters it. The man _____ because he is a _____ and cares nothing for the sheep."

Look again at verses 14 and 15.

The bond between the shepherd and the flock was similar to that of a father and his family. The shepherd in the ancient Near East would lead his flock to pasture and water, tend to their wounds, guide them, calm them, keep them together, and rescue them from pitfalls and briar patches. He was the sole provider of all that the flock needed.

How does the image of God leading you with His voice as opposed to driving you with a barking dog shape your view of God's guidance?

A
P
P
L
Y

_____

_____

_____

The shepherd would keep the flock together by calling wandering individuals back to the fold and, when necessary, would bring hardheaded sheep back by gentle application of his staff. Should one of the sheep manage to get separated and lost, the shepherd would actively seek that lost sheep until it was found—just like a loving father.

David, a shepherd himself, described this beautifully in one of the most often-quoted passages in the entire Bible: **Psalm 23.**

Read **Psalm 23** in its entirety, and then write verses 1-4, word-for-word, below. (Keep a bookmark in John 10, though. We're coming back here in a bit).

_____

_____

_____

_____

_____

_____

_____

_____

As we already learned, the shepherd used the rod with gentle application to guide and comfort the sheep—he did not strike the sheep with the rod. In fact, in shepherding, the rod was also used for counting, guiding, rescuing, and protecting the sheep.[3]

With that in mind, let's look at a related passage. Read **Proverbs 13:24** below:

"Whoever spares the rod hates their children, but the one who loves their children is careful to discipline them."

How does this information about the proper use of the rod shape your view of God's discipline?

_____

_____

A P P L Y

If you are a parent, you may recognize that verse as a justification to spank children. Knowing what you know now, how might you practically apply this knowledge about the use of the rod to the discipline of your children?

_____

_____

_____

_____

The Prophet Isaiah also spoke of God as a shepherd.

Read **Isaiah 40:1-11** and then write **Isaiah 40:11** here, word-for-word:

_____

_____

_____

_____

_____

Let's look at one more use of the shepherd/sheep metaphor in the Old Testament.

Read **Jeremiah 31:10** in your Bible and complete the verse below:

"Hear the word of the Lord, you nations; proclaim it in distant coastlands: 'He who scattered Israel will _____

_____

_____ ...,'

Now, turn back to **John 10.**

What does Jesus repeatedly say He does for the sheep in verses 11, 15, and 17-18?

_____

The phrase used in these verses "give his life for" literally means "a voluntary, sacrificial death" and is only found in the writings of John. (**John 10:11, John 10:15; John 10:17-18; John 13:37-38; John 15:13; 1 John 3:16** [twice])

In sheep herding, a good shepherd would risk his own life to save the sheep from any dangerous situation, including those brought on by the sheep itself. Should a predator attack the flock, the shepherd would willingly give his life to protect his sheep.

One of the most striking examples of this is found in **I Samuel 17:34-37.** Read this passage in your Bible and describe it in your own words:

_____

_____

_____

_____

_____

Take a moment and thank Jesus for giving His life, voluntarily and sacrificially, to protect us and save us. Feel free to write out a prayer of gratitude.

_____

_____

_____

_____

_____

Finally, let's go back and look at the verses we skipped, **John 10: 6-10.**

In verse 10, what are the three things the thief comes to the pen to do?

———————————— , ———————————— , ————————————

We often hear that verse quoted about Satan — *Satan* comes to steal, kill, and destroy. I've stated that verse in the same way, right up until about five minutes ago when I studied it in context.

While Satan is, in fact, a thief (stealing our joy, peace, innocence, resources, etc.), Jesus was not talking about Satan in this passage.

Look back at **Ezekiel 34:1-10,** and then **John 10:1 and 8.** Based on these verses, who do you think the "thief" is that Jesus was talking about in verse 10?

_____

_____

_____

What does Jesus call Himself in verses 7 and 9?

_____

I have always been confused about why Jesus called himself "the shepherd" in some places and "the gate" in others. Shouldn't He be one or the other? How can He be both?

Then, as I studied, I learned something about the shepherd that not only clarified these statements, but also completely wrecked me: When the sheep would return to the fold at night after a day of grazing, the shepherd would stand in the doorway of the pen and physically inspect each sheep as it entered. He would anoint any sheep who were scratched or wounded and give water to those who were thirsty.

Then, after all the sheep had been counted and brought back into the pen, the shepherd would *lay down across the doorway* so that no intruder—human or beast—could enter without his knowledge. The shepherd literally became the door of the pen, the protector, the sole determiner of who entered the fold and who was excluded. This is why Jesus claimed to be both the shepherd and the gate.[4]

As I consider the imagery of these loving and selfless actions of the shepherd, I'm remembering the many times I have inspected my own babies from head to toe, fed them, held them tightly after a long, hard day, tended to their wounds, and quenched their thirst. During one particularly scary night, I literally slept on the hard floor across the threshold of the bedroom of my sick child.

The gate... I get it now.

When I think about the Shepherd leading me and feeding me, searching for me when I'm lost and snatching me from the pit, inspecting me and tending to my wounds, calming me and keeping me together, then literally lying down to guard and protect me... This blows my mind. I want to know this Shepherd. I want to recognize the sound of His voice. When He calls me by name, I want to follow.

FOR DISCUSSION

❋   Look back over what you learned in this lesson. What role or duty of
the Shepherd is the most meaningful to you right now? Why?

_____

_____

_____

_____

_____

_____

_____

_____

_____

_____

_____

_____

_____

_____

_____

_____

_____

_____

❋   What do you want to learn in this study? Why are you working through this particular study right now? In what ways do you want to see growth by the time it is finished?

_____

_____

_____

_____

_____

_____

_____

_____

_____

_____

_____

_____

_____

_____

_____

_____

_____

✦   What was your biggest takeaway from this lesson?

_____

_____

_____

_____

_____

_____

_____

_____

_____

_____

_____

_____

_____

_____

_____

_____

_____

_____

_____

_____

_____

_____

Lesson Two

How God Speaks

AN OVERVIEW OF GOD'S MOTIVES AND METHODS

"In the beginning, God created the heavens and the earth. Now the earth was formless and empty, darkness was over the surface of the deep, and the Spirit of God was hovering over the waters. And God said…"

GENESIS 1:1-3A

When I first suspected God was speaking to me, it went a little something like this:

I would be praying in my family room, kneeling in front of our plush, overstuffed, brown recliner (home décor, circa 1998), when suddenly, a thought, phrase, or scripture would enter my mind. Then, a few hours or even days later, I would be listening to the radio or maybe sitting in church listening to a sermon, and the person speaking would say the exact same thought, phrase, or scripture. Sometimes, I'd hear it in more than one place over a few days. And I'd think to myself, *Hey, I was just praying about that. What a coincidence. Wait… was it just a coincidence? Or was it God? Or maybe I didn't pray that exact thing at all… never mind.*

In the early days of praying and asking God to teach me to discern His voice, this scenario played out more and more frequently.

Then one morning, I poured my heart out to God about all the deep, personal things that concerned me. Suddenly, my mind was flooded with not one, but multiple phrases, words, and portions of Scripture. I opened my Bible and, using the concordance in the back, searched for every one of those phrases, words, and portions of Scripture. I was astounded by the way each verse specifically addressed my prayers and concerns.

I considered that maybe my brain was simply recalling relevant information from the Rolodex of my memory. (Rolodex: apparently, I'm hopelessly stuck in the 90s.) I also thought that maybe this was actually what God's voice sounded like when He spoke. Perhaps it was a combination of both those things. I mostly hoped it was God's voice.

That morning, I decided to journal everything I thought God was speaking to me—every scripture, every phrase, every keyword—all of it. I wrote the words: "This is what I think God is saying to me." I had never written a "God said" sort of entry in my journal before. I felt foolish doing it. I worried someone would read it and think I was a freak. (Side note: my daughter was two-years-old, and my husband had always preferred "perusing" to reading—even when I'd send him an email with vital details that he should actually read—so the chances of someone reading this journal entry were precisely zero.)

I ended that prayer time with a sincere request for God to confirm His voice in any way He saw fit—if, in fact, it was His voice.

The next night I headed out to hear my friend, Renee, speak at a women's ministry event. Renee is a Bible teacher and a lover of God's word. I had the privilege of sitting under her teaching in an adult Sunday school class for about a year prior to that night. I had been mesmerized by her extensive Bible knowledge and passion for God. She had a zeal for the Lord that made a distinct impression on my heart as a young woman.

Every time Renee prayed for me, she prayed with wisdom and insight that was beyond her actual knowledge of my circumstances. God had used her many times to speak encouragement to me. So, while I didn't understand how God would confirm His voice to me, I was hopeful He'd use Renee or someone like her to do it. (We will talk more about hearing God through other people in Lesson Eight.)

I sat down and opened my journal to the pages where I recorded my fragments and thoughts and Scriptural references. Then, with pen in hand, I opened my heart to see what God would say to me.

At the risk of sounding like a click-bait title from a cheesy Internet article, you won't believe what happened next!

Every single scripture, every single keyword, and every single phrase God spoke to me in my prayer time the previous morning, God also spoke through Renee at some point that evening. I would have counted it as a coincidence if she had referenced one or two of them—but all of them? I believe this was the confirmation I was seeking. I still have that journal, with all my scribbles writing "CONFIRMATION" in the margin.

After that night, I knew I was onto something. God was speaking to me, and I could hear Him.

I'm saying that all chill, like it was no big deal. *It's just God speaking to me. Whatevs.*

So, let me be crystal clear: I was awestruck. GOD WAS SPEAKING TO ME, AND I COULD HEAR HIM!

The pursuit of hearing God and knowing His voice was bearing fruit. From that night on, it took on new life.

For the next several months, still praying in my living room in and around our big, brown chair, I regularly asked God to help me hear Him clearly and often. For fear that I would be led astray or deceived, I would also ask God to confirm His voice to me in some way.

❧

One night during that season of pursuit, I went to our church to hear a guest minister preach. He was a man I had never met from a Latin

American country I had never visited. He spoke very broken English and required a translator to preach.

From the beginning of the sermon, this man's prophetic gift was apparent. I had never seen anything like it before. He was calling men and women in the congregation forward so he could pray for them. And when he did, he'd encourage them about specific things God was doing in them and through them. I knew many of the people and their situations personally, and his prayers and words of encouragement were accurate. It wasn't creepy or tacky. It didn't have the icky feeling of a flashy televangelist manipulating gullible church-folk. His prayers were beautiful, quiet, and reverent. Tears streamed down my face the entire night as I listened to God speak through that soft-spoken, humble servant of God.

Fascinated that God was speaking to others, but disappointed that He hadn't yet spoken to me, I decided to head home. Jon was there watching our babies, one of whom was a newborn. It was late, and I was severely sleep-deprived. The service continued, while I quietly slipped out of my seat and headed to the back door of our small church.

Just before I could exit the building, I felt someone's hand on my arm. I turned around and was surprised to see this minister trying to catch me before I left. In very broken English, he looked me in the eye and spoke these words:

"You hear the voice of God. When you are praying in your living room by the chair at night, He speaks to you, and you hear Him."

Um. You guys.

Yes, I am very aware this sounds like a fake story. After it first happened, I replayed it in my head numerous times, wondering if there was some way that guest minister knew what I prayed or where I prayed (in front of a chair?!) or how desperately I needed to hear exactly those words of confirmation.

Nope. It actually happened exactly as I described. And I have dozens of additional personal examples in my life that are just as profound.

I'm thankful the examples of God speaking to people don't begin and end with me, though. The Bible is one giant testimony to the fact that He speaks to people—clearly, deliberately, and undeniably.

Literally, the very first action we see in Scripture is God speaking:

"In the beginning, God created the heavens and the earth. Now the earth was formless and empty, darkness was over the surface of the deep, and the Spirit of God was hovering over the waters. **And God said...**"

Genesis 1:1-3a (emphasis mine)

Look up **Psalm 33:6** in your Bible and fill in the blanks regarding God speaking creation into existence:

"By _____ the heavens were made, the starry host, by _____ ."

And all the way at the end of the Bible, in the final book, we see Jesus offering this invitation to hear His voice:

"Here I am! I stand at the door and knock. If anyone **hears my voice** *and opens the door, I will come in and eat with that person, and they with me."* **Revelation 3:20 (emphasis mine)**

So, let's spend this lesson taking an in-depth look at some of the unique ways God spoke between Genesis and Revelation. But first, we'll identify why God speaks in the first place.

GOD'S COMMUNICATION GOALS AND MOTIVES

When I had little ones at home, buried in toys and laundry (me, not my little ones), I'd meet my husband at the door at dinnertime, and for the next couple hours, I'd talk. And talk. And talk. I'd talk about nothing and about everything. I scarcely took a breath; I was desperate for intelligent, adult conversation. After answering toddler questions and reading rhyming storybooks all day, I had a surplus of adult words I needed to use by the end of the night. I'd tell Jon, "I just need to process."

God is not like that. (Neither is my husband, by the way.) God's not just speaking for the heck of it. He's not bored. He doesn't need to "process." God's words are always deliberate and specific. **He always has a purpose when He speaks.**

As we look at the various Biblical examples of God speaking in this lesson and throughout this study, we will see God's purpose fall into one or more of these categories, understanding much overlap exists in these purposes and God probably has more that I have yet to identify:

* **God wants you to know the truth about who He is.**

* **God wants you to know the truth about who you are.**

* **God wants you to know the truth about others and who they are.**

* **God wants you to know what to do to further His kingdom.**

* **God wants to tell you how and why to avoid sin (and whether or not you're in sin).**

* **God wants to tell you what He is doing.**

* **God wants your heart to be transformed into His image.**

* **God wants you to glorify His name.**

Understanding God's motives is integral to understanding His voice. We may hear Him on occasion, but sometimes cannot correctly interpret and apply what we hear. Knowing *why* God speaks to His people not only helps us discern the voices to determine if it's God speaking, but it also helps us correctly apply what we know to be a word from the Lord. If you think you hear something from God, run it through those eight filters and see if it makes sense. If it doesn't fit, it's probably not God speaking.

REFLECT AND ASSESS Can you think of a time that you thought God was speaking to you? Can you identify what His goal or motive was in saying what He said? Describe what you think He said and then choose whatever goals/motives apply. (It's okay if you can't think of anything; we're only on Lesson Two, after all.)

_____

_____

_____

_____

_____

_____

GOD'S METHODS

In addition to having motives or reasons to speak, God also has methods in which He speaks. At the end of this lesson we will look at several of them in the Bible. Some of the methods God used repeatedly. Others we only see once in Scripture. This tells us that

- God can speak however He wants, to whomever He wants, however He wants. The key is not *how* God spoke, but *that* He spoke.

- We can confidently look to certain methods as the primary or most common ways God speaks, as they are used multiple (sometimes hundreds!) of times.

Here is an overview of the primary methods God uses to speak. I will cover the first three in greater detail throughout the remainder of this Bible study:

GOD SPEAKS THROUGH SCRIPTURE

This is *the* primary way and also the standard against which we measure everything else we hear. The Bible is literally God's word—His voice in written form. As I stated in the Introduction, I don't have space in this

Bible study to examine all the reasons why Christians trust the Scriptures to be the word of God. So if you have doubts, I encourage you to set this Bible study aside and first explore the authority of Scripture on your own. You will have a very difficult time discerning the voice of God if you don't first establish this premise in your own heart and mind.

GOD SPEAKS THROUGH THE INNER VOICE

After God speaking to you directly through the written word of God, the next most common method is God speaking directly to your heart. Of all the methods, it causes the most confusion. I have a steady monologue going on in my mind, and it's sometimes difficult to figure out who's talking. I don't think I'm alone here, since the number-one question I get from people on the topic of hearing God is, "Is the voice in my head God or just me?" (Thus, the title of this Bible study.)

GOD SPEAKS THROUGH OTHER PEOPLE

God often uses other people to speak to us, either directly, or through sermons, books, prophecy, songs, etc. As you probably suspect, not all people who claim to hear God on our behalf are actually hearing God on our behalf—and if you don't suspect this, you should. If you recall, confusion over this method is precisely why I began studying the topic of hearing God's voice over 20 years ago.

The remaining methods are also common, but I'm not devoting an entire lesson to them, because I have so much other material I want to cover with you in this study. We'll touch briefly on each one and then I'll give you an opportunity to dig deeper on your own.

GOD SPEAKS THROUGH CIRCUMSTANCES/OPEN AND CLOSED DOORS

Christians are all over the map on how to interpret circumstances with regard to God's will. I've heard some people say that if things are going too smoothly you must be doing something wrong. And others say that if things are going too smoothly you're doing something right. So, which is it?

The short answer: it's both.

God can and will manipulate circumstances to direct your path. He opens doors. He closes doors. He will use anything and anyone He chooses to accomplish His purpose. He neither requests nor requires permission to move things around to accomplish His will. But here's the thing: people can also manipulate circumstances! Without some discernment on our part, it's hard to know the difference. But one thing's clear in Scripture: When God opens a door—literal or figurative—no one can shut it.

In **Revelation 3:7-8**, Jesus says,

"To the angel of the church in Philadelphia write:

These are the words of him who is holy and true, who holds the key of David. **What he opens no one can shut, and what he shuts no one can open.** I know your deeds. See, **I have placed before you an open door that no one can shut.** I know that you have little strength, yet you have kept my word and have not denied my name." (Emphasis mine)

In your Bible, read the following passages regarding circumstances where God opened literal doors that no one could shut.

Joshua 5:13-6:27

What "door" opened? Why?

_____

_____

Acts 12:1-18

What door opened? Why?

_____

_____

If only our open doors (or fallen walls) were always that obvious. Most of the time, though, the doors we encounter are figurative, not literal—an opportunity or loss of one, the beginning or end of a relationship, financial gain or loss—and the purpose of them in our lives, ambiguous.

Jon and I have relocated across the country three times. As with all major decisions, relocating affects countless people, so we have always sought to acquire a large degree of certainty that it was God's leading before uprooting our family and replanting elsewhere. Every time we moved, God started lining up circumstances to guide us in that direction months ahead of time. We didn't recognize it as such, especially at the beginning. Before we left Florida and moved to Kentucky, Jon and I both sensed that something was about to change. We weren't sure what, but we both had the urge to "move on." At first we thought maybe it just meant a house-move or a church-move. But as the weeks unfolded, circumstances indicated it was more like a *move-move*. Jon felt stuck in his job. A babysitting gig I had taken was coming to an end. The Bible study I was teaching was drawing to a close. Rebekah was about to enter into kindergarten, marking a natural transition into the next season of parenting. Everything that tethered us to Florida was lifting at the same time, positioning us to relocate. It wasn't long before Jon was offered a great job, and all of the circumstances made sense. (Because without all that, moving from Florida to Kentucky makes no sense. At least to me.)

But circumstances alone don't always indicate God's will. Sometimes circumstances contradict one another.

In your Bible, read **I Corinthians 16:5-9**, and write out verse 9 word-for-word:

_____

_____

Here we see Paul walking through the "open door" despite great opposition from the people in the area. He had an open door from God but, what appeared to be, a closed door from the people.

Now read **2 Corinthians 2:12-13** in your Bible.

Was this an open door or a closed door?

_____

What contrary circumstance to the open/closed door did Paul face?

_____

_____

_____

What did Paul do?

_____

_____

_____

Here we see the Lord opening another door of opportunity for ministry, but Paul rejects it. This is interesting, isn't it? If God opened a door for Paul, why wouldn't he feel peace? Write your thoughts here. (It's okay if you don't know. I'll be honest, I don't understand this myself. When I don't understand something in God's word, I like to write my questions out to God and ask Him directly. I invite you to do the same.):

_____

_____

_____

Now read a parable Jesus told in **Luke 18:1-8** and write verse 1 word-for-word:

_____

_____

_____

Here we see a closed door that Jesus encourages us to try to open with persistent prayer.

REFLECT AND ASSESS

Are there any closed doors in your life that you are praying for God to open?

_____

_____

_____

SUMMARY

⚙ Sometimes God opens literal and figurative doors that no man can shut.

⚙ Sometimes God opens a door and gives us the freedom to accept or reject the invitation.

⚙ Sometimes people can manipulate circumstances and confuse God's plans.

⚙ Sometimes a series of open doors will lead you to God's will.

⚙ Sometimes the door is closed, but God wants you to persist in prayer to open it.

Tricky, right? This is why circumstances should never be interpreted independent of God's word, inner peace, and godly counsel (the three primary methods). If you are unsure about whether God is speaking to you through your circumstances, go back to God's word first and compare it to what the Bible says. Pay attention to what you are hearing in your spirit. Seek godly counsel. There is no formula to any of this. It requires diligence and time—time to seek clarification, yes. But mostly, time to get to know God.

Henry Blackaby says it best:

> "The problem with open doors is the emphasis is erroneously placed on the door rather than on God... Looking for open doors can appear easier than developing a relationship with God... If decision-making were based entirely on open doors, people would not need a relationship with God: they could merely become "door watchers."[6]

DIG DEEPER: One of the most beautiful stories of God using circumstances to lead someone and accomplish His will—often very difficult or seemingly impossible circumstances—is that of Joseph. Take some time to read the story of Joseph from beginning to end. Take note of all the opened and closed doors God used to steer Joseph where He wanted him to go. The story is found in Genesis chapters 37-47. (Just a reminder, these Dig Deeper sections are intended for you to complete only if you'd like to read additional Scripture related to, but not necessarily covered in, this study. If you want to move past these or come back to this at the end of the entire study, feel free.)

GOD SPEAKS THROUGH NATURE

When I was a new Christian, I thought people who said they felt close to God in nature were New Age freaks. (I can be real with you, right?) I thought "being in nature" was a cop-out for getting in the Bible and dropping to your knees and praying like a REAL Christian (said in my best Dana Carvey Church Lady voice). Obviously, I had much to learn about God, His word, and His voice.

Today, God often speaks to me through nature. To me there is nothing more sacred than standing at the shoreline and looking across the ocean, listening to the roar of the waves (which is highly inconvenient while living in Kentucky!). That's why the beach is my favorite place—it reminds me of my smallness and God's bigness.

Thankfully, the sky does the same thing for me. (Kentucky has no ocean, but it does have a sky!) In the morning when I drive my kids to school, we often look at the sunrise together. I have been known to actually pull off to the side of the road to watch it. When my kids were little, I would talk to them about how creative God is and how He loves to give us beautiful things. I would remind them that no other sunrise will ever look exactly like the one God is giving us right now. I would tell them that God gave us today's sunrise for our pleasure and enjoyment, simply because He loves us and wants to see us smile. When I am writing or working on a podcast and feel like I'm running out of ideas, I often remember the sunrise—how it's different every single day. I remember the Creator of the sunrise, in all His limitless creativity, is also the Creator of me. And I happen to be created in His image. This means that I never have to worry about running out of ideas.

1. In your Bible, find **Psalm 19:1-2** and write it here, word-for-word.

_____

_____

_____

_____

2. God speaks to everyone through nature—even to the ungodly and the unrighteous. Look at **Romans 1:18-20 (ESV)** below:

18 For the wrath of God is revealed from heaven against all ungodliness and unrighteousness of men, who by their unrighteousness suppress the truth. **19** For what can be known about God is plain to them, because God has shown it to them. **20** For his invisible attributes, namely, his eternal power and divine nature, have been clearly perceived, ever since the creation of the world, in the things that have been made. So they are without excuse.

What specifically does God reveal about Himself to the ungodly through nature? (v. 20)

_____

_____

3. Jesus pointed his disciples toward nature to understand God's character. In your Bible read **Luke 12:22-31**

What elements of nature did Jesus point them (us!) to?

_____

What do you think this reveals about God?

_____

_____

_____

4. Two of the most notable instances where God spoke through nature are found in the following passages. Find them in your Bible and answer the accompanying questions.

Genesis 9:8-17

What element of nature did God use to speak?

_____

What did God say through that element?

_____

_____

_____

Mark 15:25-37

What element of nature did God use to speak? (v. 33)

_____

What did God say through that element?

_____

_____

_____

SUMMARY

❋   Throughout Scripture God speaks to people through nature.

❋   God speaks to both the righteous and the unrighteous this way, so that everyone has an opportunity to see and hear God.

❋   Through nature, God reveals His character—beauty, might, intelligence, attention to detail, and creativity without limit. He reminds us of his covenant with us. He reminds us of His commitment to us to supply our needs. He establishes that He alone is God.

GOD SPEAKS THROUGH DREAMS AND VISIONS

Two weeks after my nine-month-old son Noah died, I was in his bedroom holding his blanket, rocking slowly in the rocking chair, and weeping. I know this goes without saying, but losing my son was the worst pain I had ever endured in my entire life, before or since, hands-down. I simply have no words to describe the despair I was in at that moment.

The phone rang and a woman from church called to see how I was doing. I told her I was in Noah's room rocking and crying, and she said, "You need to get out of there." *What? Such an odd and insensitive thing to say,* I thought. Even as I type this, my heart aches, because I was alone in my house and I missed my baby so, so much... I was just sitting in the place where I felt closest to him.

I know she meant well. I get that now. She was trying to encourage me to get up and do something else that wasn't so, well, *sad.* (Note: Everything was sad. I could have done nothing differently to make me less sad.) I thanked her for her concern, but told her I was just going to sit there for now. She argued with me—insisted that I get up and resist my sorrow because I was fighting a spiritual battle or something. I don't remember exactly the point she was trying to make or how I responded, except I remember regretting that I had answered the phone. The conversation rapidly deteriorated, and at one point she said something ridiculous like, "I think Satan took your baby."

(Ugh. I know.)

(It's fine. I'm fine. This story has a point, and it's not "what not to say to a grieving mother".)

(Though, if I were to advise one on this topic, "Satan took your baby" would be at the top of the list of things NOT to say.)

In an effort to believe the best about this woman, she and my entire church family were trying to make sense of Noah's death. This particular woman faithfully prayed for Noah and his healing. Without getting off on a tangent about a particular church doctrine right now, she sincerely believed that our faith (hers included) should have been sufficient to heal Noah—that physical healing was and always is God's will. When Noah died, she was looking for another explanation. Enter: "Satan took your baby."

As you can probably imagine, I ended the phone call abruptly. I literally fell on the floor sobbing. I screamed out to God in desperation and anger and exhaustion and anguish, "Lord, if Satan is able to take a child like Noah—a child covered in prayer from conception and bathed in the Word every single day of his life, a child prayed for by literally tens of thousands of people around the world... If Satan has that much power to snatch my child, then please, if You have any shred of compassion for me, please, do not give me any more children. I don't want them if it means You aren't able to protect them from Satan's power. Please tell me now, one way or another, if Satan took my son. Because if he did, I'm never having another child again as long as I live."

At that exact moment, the phone rang again.

(Keep in mind; this was 1998, before caller ID). I was afraid "Satan-took-your-baby lady" was calling back for more "words of encouragement." I had no desire to talk to anyone. But I felt God nudge me to answer it anyway.

I did. It was my sister-in-law. She asked how I was doing and I proceeded to spew out everything that had just happened—the phone call, the insensitive comments, the prayer I had just prayed, all of it. I'm quite sure I was incoherent, what with all the sobbing and heaving.

And she said, "Well, that explains why God told me to call you just now. Last week I was praying for you, and I was saying to God, 'This is terrible, Lord. There is nothing good about this.' And God said, 'It's not terrible. You only saw Noah die with your physical eyes, but let Me show you what was happening in the Spirit.'"

She said suddenly she saw the hospital room, just as it was when Noah died. All of us were there, the doctors were trying to resuscitate him, nurses were scurrying around, Jon and I were crying—the whole scene. Then suddenly, the room changed. She said, "Sandy, every single place you had prayed that week for an angel to be, it was there. There were angels that looked like guards at his door. There was a line of blood on the floor where you prayed the blood of Jesus to be. There were angels hovering over his bed. They were everywhere. And Jesus was standing by Noah's bedside with His hand on Noah's chest, and Noah was looking into Jesus' eyes and he was smiling. Noah asked Jesus, 'Is it time yet?' and Jesus, said, 'Not yet'. And then just as the doctors walked out of the room to say, 'I'm sorry, we've done everything we can do', Jesus picked Noah up, and Noah laid his head on Jesus' shoulder, and Jesus carried him out of the room."

She went on to say, "I wanted to call you and tell you about this vision last week, but God said, 'No'. I was just sitting here and it was like an alarm went off and God said, 'Call her right now. Call her right now and tell her the vision.'"

Then she said, "Sandy, Satan didn't take your baby. His death was a holy moment to God."

God gave my sister-in-law the vision before I even uttered (screamed) the prayer. He sent me the exact thing I needed at the exact time. Not only that, but unbeknownst to me at the time, I was already pregnant with my daughter, Rebekah. Because of that vision and my sister-in-law's obedience to call me at the precise moment I needed it, I would go on to walk in faith throughout that pregnancy, and I'd never again question God's ability to protect my children from the hand of Satan.

Dreams and visions are not typical for me, but I have clearly benefited from the dreams and visions of others. God told the prophet Joel He would speak to people this way.

In your Bible, read **Joel 2:28-32** and complete verses 28-29:

And afterward, I will pour out my Spirit on _____.
Your sons and daughters will _____ , your
old men will _____ , your young men will
_____ . Even on my servants, both men
and women, I will pour out my Spirit in those days.

DIG DEEPER: This prophecy of Joel's was fulfilled on the Day of Pentecost. In your Bible read Acts Chapter 1 and 2 to see the fulfillment of the prophecy and the subsequent birth of the Church.

SUMMARY

List the six ways we've covered so far that God speaks to people:

1. _____

2. _____

3. _____

4. _____

5. _____

6. _____

Now let's look at a series of examples showing God speaking to people in a variety of ways. Most of the time in the Bible—over 1,500 times—when describing God speaking, it simply says, "God said," "the Lord said," or "God spoke." It isn't clear if God spoke audibly or directly to the heart. The first example below fits this description. Other times God spoke in profound and sometimes humorous ways. (I cannot read Numbers 22 without giggling.) The passages I've selected below are a good sampling of these various methods.

For each of the examples that follow, read the portion of Scripture where God spoke and answer a few questions about the incident. Though it's time-consuming, I highly recommend you read the entire chapter where the passage appears to help you with the context, even if you are familiar with the story. I've completed the first one for you.

OLD TESTAMENT EXAMPLES

1. Genesis 2:15-17

To whom was God speaking? *Adam*

What method did God use to speak? *It simply says, "He commanded the man." So we are not sure.*

Why did God speak? *God wanted Adam to know what to do. (Reference the eight communication goals for your answer to this question, noting that there may be more than one reason.)*

What is God saying to me? *(If a verse stands out to you, or if you sense God giving you specific direction or insight, write it here. If not, leave it blank.)*

Now your turn...

2. Genesis 16:7-12

To whom was God speaking?

_____

What method did God use to speak?

_____

Why did God speak?

_____

What is God saying to me?

_____

3. Genesis 18:1-15

To whom was God speaking?

_____

What method did God use to speak?

_____

Why did God speak?

_____

What is God saying to me?

_____

4. Genesis 28:10-20

To whom was God speaking?

_____

What method did God use to speak?

_____

Why did God speak?

_____

What is God saying to me?

_____

5. Exodus 3:1-4:14

To whom was God speaking?

_____

What method did God use to speak?

_____

Why did God speak? (Look for multiple reasons here)

_____

What is God saying to me?

_____

DIG DEEPER: Want to keep going? Continue with the remaining Old Testament examples. Otherwise, skip to the New Testament examples that follow.

6. Numbers 22:28-35

To whom was God speaking?

_____

What method did God use to speak? (Look for two methods here.)

_____

Why did God speak?

_____

What is God saying to me?

_____

7. I Samuel 3:1-14

To whom was God speaking?

_____

What method did God use to speak?

_____

Why did God speak?

_____

What is God saying to me?

_____

8. I Kings 19:5-18

To whom was God speaking?

_____

What method did God use to speak? (Look for more than one.)

_____

Why did God speak?

_____

What is God saying to me?

_____

9. Job 38:1-3

To whom was God speaking?

_____

What method did God use to speak?

_____

Why did God speak? (God's questions to Job go on for 4 chapters (!), but can you determine one main reason God was speaking to Job in this situation?)

_____

What is God saying to me?

_____

10. Isaiah 6:1-8

To whom was God speaking?

_____

What method did God use to speak?

_____

Why did God speak?

_____

What is God saying to me?

_____

IN THE NEW TESTAMENT

The most direct, profound, and miraculous way God has ever spoken is through the mouth and life of Jesus Christ. God became man and walked on this earth with a physical body, talking to people with an actual voice. Thankfully, we still have written record of many of Jesus' words. They are as relevant today as they were 2,000 years ago. You can read through the four Gospels (Matthew, Mark, Luke, and John) to learn what He said as recorded by the people who heard it. In many Bibles, the publisher prints Jesus' words in red.

Before Jesus' birth and after His death and resurrection, God continued to speak in other ways. Here are a few examples.

1. Matthew 1:20-24 and 2:12

To whom was God speaking?

_____

What method did God use to speak?

_____

Why did God speak?

_____

What is God saying to me?

_____

2. Matthew 3:1-17

To whom was God speaking?

_____

What method did God use to speak?

_____

Why did God speak?

_____

What is God saying to me?

_____

3. Luke 1:11-20

To whom was God speaking?

_____

What method did God use to speak?

_____

Why did God speak?

_____

What is God saying to me?

_____

4. Luke 1:26-38

To whom was God speaking?

_____

What method did God use to speak?

_____

Why did God speak?

_____

What is God saying to me?

_____

5. Acts 9:1-9

To whom was God speaking?

_____

What method did God use to speak?

_____

Why did God speak?

_____

What is God saying to me?

_____

 DIG DEEPER: Want to keep going? Continue working through the remaining New Testament examples.

6. Acts 9:10-18

To whom was God speaking?

_____

What method did God use to speak?

_____

Why did God speak?

_____

What is God saying to me?

_____

7. Acts 10:1-7

To whom was God speaking?

_____

What method did God use to speak?

_____

Why did God speak?

_____

What is God saying to me?

_____

8. Acts 10:9-16

To whom was God speaking?

_____

What method did God use to speak?

_____

Why did God speak?

_____

What is God saying to me?

_____

Finally, look back over all you've studied in this lesson (well done, by the way). Have you learned anything new?

_____

_____

_____

_____

_____

_____

_____

The examples we studied here barely scratch the surface concerning the number of Biblical accounts of God speaking. Maybe believing that God spoke in the Bible has never been an issue for you, so this lesson affirmed what you already knew. Or maybe you have a disconnection between God speaking *to a Bible character* and God speaking *to you*. Or perhaps you believe that God will speak to you, *but only through the Bible*. These are legitimate positions. I will try to address those as thoroughly as possible in the remainder of this study.

"God's choice to communicate in so many diverse ways forces us to put our faith in him, not a method. We do not seek a word from God to prove he is real so we can have a relationship with him. Rather, as we seek to develop an intimate relationship with him, we will hear him speak to us."
Henry Blackaby[7]

As we wrap up this lesson, with all these Biblical examples still fresh in our minds, and the majority of this Bible study still ahead of us, let me leave you with a quote from John Eldredge:

> *"Now, I know, I know—the prevailing belief is that God speaks to his people only through the Bible. And let me make this clear: he does speak to us first and foremost through the Bible. That is the basis for our relationship. The Bible is the eternal and unchanging Word of God to us. It is such a gift, to have right there in black and white God's thoughts toward us. We know right off the bat that any other supposed revelation from God that contradicts the Bible is not to be trusted. So I am not minimizing in any way the authority of the Scripture or the fact that God speaks to us through the Bible.*
>
> *However, many Christians believe that God only speaks to us through the Bible.*
>
> *The irony of that belief is that's not what the Bible says...*
>
> *Now, if God doesn't also speak to us, why would he have given us all these stories of him speaking to others? 'Look—here are hundreds of inspiring and hopeful stories about how God spoke to his people in this and that situation. Isn't it amazing? But you can't have that. He doesn't speak like that anymore.' That makes no sense at all. Why would God give you a book of exceptions? This is how I used to relate to my people, but I don't do that anymore. What good would a book of exceptions do you?*
>
> *No, the Bible is a book of examples of what it looks like to walk with God. To say that he doesn't offer that to us is just so disheartening. It is also unbiblical."*[8]

FOR DISCUSSION

* Why do you think we have such a difficult time hearing God's voice if people in the Bible appeared to have no problems?

_____

_____

_____

_____

_____

_____

_____

_____

_____

_____

_____

_____

_____

_____

_____

_____

_____

_____

_____

Do you believe you have the potential to hear God as clearly as those in Biblical times? Why or why not?

_____

_____

_____

_____

_____

_____

_____

_____

_____

_____

_____

_____

_____

_____

_____

_____

_____

_____

_____

_____

✿   What do you think about Eldredge's affirmation that "it makes no sense" to have a book of "exceptions"? Agree or disagree? Why or why not?

_____

_____

_____

_____

_____

_____

_____

_____

_____

_____

_____

_____

_____

_____

_____

_____

_____

_____

_____

What is your biggest takeaway from this lesson?

_____

_____

_____

_____

_____

_____

_____

_____

_____

_____

_____

_____

_____

_____

_____

_____

_____

_____

_____

_____

_____

Lesson Three

Introducing The 5 Keys to Becoming a Good Listener

CULTIVATE A GROWING RELATIONSHIP WITH GOD
SATURATE YOUR MIND WITH SCRIPTURE

> *"Incline your ear [to listen] and come to Me; Hear, so that your soul may live;"*

ISAIAH 55:3 (AMP)

My son loves to walk around with music in his ears at all times. Part fashion statement, part distraction, he's rarely without an apparatus in or over his ears to drown out the noise and voices around him. His favorite is a set of noise-canceling headphones. He sometimes keeps them on even when the music is off. This conspicuous and clunky piece of technology says to the world, "Don't talk to me." As his mother, who sometimes needs to talk to him, this doesn't always work for me. He swears he can still hear me with them on (Um…something about "noise-canceling" tells me otherwise). He's looking at me, but his body language is telling me, "I'm not listening to you." He may as well be standing in front of me with his hands over his ears.

Yesterday, as Elijah sat at the computer in the dining room with his headphones on, Jon tried to ask him a question. Jon started by calling out Elijah's name from across the room. No response. Then he moved closer and called a little louder. Still nothing. Then Jon literally stood directly behind Elijah and yelled, "ELIJAH!" Elijah proceeded with his video game, unmoved.

This happens on the regular. We aren't always sure if he's faking or *for-real* cannot hear us. Sometimes, as a test, Jon and I will say in a whisper voice, "I think we should buy Elijah a brand new car." We are hilarious.

His second favorite set of headphones is a pair of small wireless earbuds. Unlike the giant noise-canceling headphones, these earbuds are barely visible and can be worn almost anywhere. Half the time, I don't know he has them in. Thus, I will often start talking to him—telling him in great detail the plans for the day, what I need him to do, my hopes and dreams for his future (I exaggerate only slightly), and he will ignore me. What first appears as utter disrespect for his mom is actually just music blaring in his barely-visible earbuds, drowning out my voice.

I don't blame him for wanting to cancel out the noise. I get it. He suffers with ADHD and Asperger's, which means normal background noise is distracting and often overwhelming to him. I don't mind him using them, for the most part. But when I'm talking to him—when I have something important to say to him, when I want to have a conversation with my son— it's a different story. I want him to look me in the eye and take the earbuds or headphones off his ears... *All the way off.* I don't care if he's turned down the music. I don't care if he's taken one earbud out. I don't care if he swears he can hear me with them on. It's important to me for him to posture himself to listen when I'm talking to him.

God feels the same way about us.

Read **Isaiah 55:2-3 (AMP)** below:

2 *"Why do you spend money for that which is not bread,*
And your earnings for what does not satisfy?
Listen carefully to Me, and eat what is good,
And let your soul delight in abundance.

3 *"Incline your ear [to listen] and come to Me;*
Hear, so that your soul may live;
And I will make an everlasting covenant with you,
According to the faithful mercies [promised and] shown to David."

Circle the phrase "incline your ear to listen" in verse 3.

The word translated as "incline" is the Hebrew word *natah.* It means to stretch forth or spread out, stretch down, or turn aside. In other translations, we see the phrase you circled translated as

Give ear and come to me; listen, (NIV)

Come to me with your ears wide open. Listen, (NLT)

Pay close attention! Come to me, (CEV)

Turn your ear, and come to me; hear, (NHEB)

Give heed with your ears, and follow my ways: hearken to me, (BST)

Natah connotes extending outward and toward something or someone. It is the same word translated outstretched in **Exodus 6:6**. Look up that verse in your Bible and write it below word-for-word:

_____

_____

_____

_____

_____

Natah also means to extend in every direction and lengthen, as in rolling out and pitching a tent; to bend down, let down, or bow; and to turn. *Natah* is active and requires effort. For example, if I *incline* to be physically healthy, I need to arrange my life to make health possible. I must educate myself about proper nutrition. I must purchase, prepare, and consume healthy food and throw away all the junk in my pantry. I must schedule time and discipline myself to get proper rest and exercise. I must learn to reduce stress. I must surround myself with people who are also seeking a healthy lifestyle. I may even need to hire a doctor, therapist, nutritionist, or personal trainer. This all takes tremendous effort and money. But when I arrange my life in this way, I maximize my chances of succeeding in my health goals. In fact, as far as it depends on me, health is inevitable when I arrange my life to support it.

"You cannot be who and what you are unless you have a lifestyle, both internally and externally, that is designed to support that definition of self."
Dr. Phil McGraw[9]

So, when God tells us to *natah* our ear, He's asking us for us to be active listeners. To posture and position ourselves to hear. To turn toward God and lean in. It requires some effort.

Let's look at another passage before we move on. It's in the book of Habakkuk—a short prophetic book tucked within a section in the back of the Old Testament known as "The Minor Prophets." It is "minor" not because of its importance, but because of its length. If you're like me, you probably skim over this book, unless specifically directed there in a Bible reading schedule or in a Bible study, like this one.

Habakkuk was a prophet of God and his message was recorded just before the Babylonian invasion of Judah in 605 BC. In chapter one, Habakkuk asked a central question to God, "Why are you silent when the wicked overtake the righteous?" A question as relevant and valid today as it was when it was written.

Then after posing the question to God, Habakkuk says,

I will **stand** *at my watch and* **station** *myself on the ramparts; I will look to see what he will say to me, and what answer I am to give to this complaint.* **Habakkuk 2:1 (emphasis mine)**

Notice the two bolded words, "stand" and "station."

The word translated "stand" is the Hebrew word *amad*—it literally means *to take one's stand.* Here is how it's been translated in other places in the Bible: to *stand, remain, endure, take one's stand, to be in a standing attitude, to stand still, stop (moving or doing), cease, to tarry, delay, remain, continue, abide, endure, persist, be steadfast, to make a stand, hold one's ground.*

The word translated "station" is the Hebrew word *yatsab* —it means *to set or station oneself, to take one's stand.*

Here's the point: Habakkuk posed his question to God and expected God to answer. While he waited, he postured himself to hear the answer—both in body and in attitude. He inclined his ear to hear God's response.

What are some practical ways you can arrange your life, both in body and attitude, to make hearing God possible? If you're not sure, it's okay—write whatever comes to mind. We'll unpack this concept as we continue this lesson:

A
P
P _____
L
Y _____

_____

_____

_____

_____

THE PARABLE OF THE GOOD LISTENER

Read **Matthew 13:1-23** below and answer the questions that follow.

That same day Jesus went out of the house and sat by the lake. **2** *Such large crowds gathered around him that he got into a boat and sat in it, while all the people stood on the shore.* **3** *Then he told them many things in parables, saying:*

"A farmer went out to sow his seed. **4** *As he was scattering the seed, some fell along the path, and the birds came and ate it up.* **5** *Some fell on rocky places, where it did not have much soil. It sprang up quickly, because the soil was shallow.* **6** *But when the sun came up, the plants were scorched, and they withered because they had no root.* **7** *Other seed fell among thorns, which grew up and choked the plants.* **8** *Still other seed fell on good soil, where it produced a crop—a hundred, sixty or thirty times what was sown.* **9** *Whoever has ears, let them hear."*

10 *The disciples came to him and asked, "Why do you speak to the people in parables?"*

11 *He replied, "Because the knowledge of the secrets of the kingdom of heaven has been given to you, but not to them.* **12** *Whoever has will be given more, and they will have an abundance. Whoever does not have, even what they have will be taken from them.* **13** *This is why I speak to them in parables:*

"Though seeing, they do not see; though hearing, they do not hear or understand.

14*In them is fulfilled the prophecy of Isaiah:*

"'You will be ever hearing but never understanding; you will be ever seeing but never perceiving. **15** *For this people's heart has become calloused; they hardly hear with their ears, and they have closed their eyes. Otherwise they might see with their eyes, hear with their ears, understand with their hearts and turn, and I would heal them.'*

16 *But blessed are your eyes because they see, and your ears because they hear.* **17** *For truly I tell you, many prophets and righteous people longed* *to see what you see but did not see it, and to hear what you hear but did not hear it.*

18 *"Listen then to what the parable of the sower means:* **19** *When anyone hears the message about the kingdom and does not understand it, the evil one comes and snatches away what was sown in their heart. This is the seed sown along the path.* **20** *The seed falling on rocky ground refers to someone who hears the word and at once receives it with joy.* **21** *But since they have no root, they last only a short time. When trouble or persecution comes because of the word, they quickly fall away.* **22** *The seed falling among the thorns refers to someone who hears the word, but the worries of this life and the deceitfulness of wealth choke the word, making it unfruitful.* **23** *But the seed falling on good soil refers to someone who hears the word and understands it. This is the one who produces a crop, yielding a hundred, sixty or thirty times what was sown."*

Go back and underline the words "listen" and all forms of the word "hear" (hears, hearing, etc.)

How many words did you underline? _____

Explain in your own words why Jesus said he spoke in parables. (See verses 13-17)

_____

_____

_____

_____

Though this parable is probably familiar to you, stick with me through some basic questions as I help you flesh out the meaning of it, particularly as it relates to being a "good listener."

The "seed" represents _____

The "soil" represents _____

The seed sown along the path: What happens to someone when they hear the message about the kingdom, but don't understand it? (v. 19)

_____

_____

The seed falling on rocky ground: What happens during trouble or persecution when someone hears the word and receives it with joy, but has no root? (vv. 20-21)

_____

_____

The seed falling on the thorns: What are the two things mentioned in verse 22 that choke the word and make it unfruitful?

_____

_____

The seed falling on good soil: What are the two things mentioned in verse 23 that are true of the person who produces an abundant crop?

_____

_____

Go back and circle the word "understand" every time it appears.

Can you draw any conclusions about the relationship between **listening to/hearing the Word** and **understanding** the Word?

_____

_____

Write verse 9 word-for-word:

_____

We see Jesus use this phrase "Whoever has ears, let him hear," many other times in Scripture to draw attention to something particularly important. (See **Mt 11:15, 43; Mk 4:9, 23; Lk 14:35; Rev 2:11, 17, 29; 3:6, 13**). A common phrase used in sage's riddles,[10] it served as both a warning and an invitation by Jesus to His hearers to exercise their minds and grasp the spiritual significance of this and other parables, to *carefully consider the meaning of the words, and to follow through on these principles in their daily lives.*[11]

We see this concept clearly echoed in the epistle of James.

Read **James 1:22-25** below and answer the question that follows:

"**22** *Do not merely listen to the word, and so deceive yourselves. Do what it says. **23** Anyone who listens to the word but does not do what it says is like someone who looks at his face in a mirror **24** and, after looking at himself, goes away and immediately forgets what he looks like. **25** But whoever looks intently into the perfect law that gives freedom, and continues in it—not forgetting what they have heard, but doing it—they will be blessed in what they do.*"

According to James, how does a person become a good listener?

_____

_____

The Parable of The Good Listener (aka, the Sower and the Seed) is also recorded in the Gospel of Luke (See **Luke 8:4-18**). After Jesus tells the parable and explains it, he makes a concluding statement. *Fill in the blanks from Luke 8:18 below (If you are not using NIV write the verse in its entirety):*

Therefore consider carefully _____ .

Listening to God's voice and God's word is not enough. **We must consider how we listen!** So, for the remainder of this lesson and in all of Lessons Four and Five, we will uncover practical ways to *incline our ear to hear* so that we can maximize our chances of understanding God's word— so that when we hear it, we will bear fruit in our lives.

SUMMARY

- Inclining your ear means to stretch, reach, and arrange your life in such a way as to make hearing God possible.

- It may mean to maintain a "standing attitude" or "stop moving or doing" until you hear God speak.

- This often means putting into practice the necessary lifestyle changes, both internally and externally, that will maximize your chances of hearing God.

- *You must create an environment where hearing God's voice, as much as it depends on you, is inevitable.*

- *"Hearing" God's word is not enough.*

- "Understanding" is a vital component of hearing God's word, allowing it to take root and bear fruit in our lives. It is the one thing that separates the good soil from all the others.

- We deceive ourselves when we merely "listen" to the word but do not do what it says.

🔊 **Pause and Listen:** Before you move on, look back and consider everything you just read. Is God saying anything to you? Write whatever comes to mind, even if you aren't sure if the voice is God's or yours:

_____

_____

_____

_____

_____

_____

INTRODUCING THE 5 KEYS TO BECOMING A GOOD LISTENER

Positioning ourselves to hear God's voice—*inclining our ears to hear*—is an ongoing and intentional series of actions encompassing our daily thoughts and habits. In other words, this will not happen accidentally. It requires a complete lifestyle shift and our total attention.

I have learned that the following keys summarize the process of positioning myself to hear God:

The 5 Keys to Becoming a Good Listener

- **Cultivate a Growing Relationship with God**
- **Saturate Your Mind with Scripture**
- **Integrate Periods of Solitude**
- **Emulate a Spirit of Humility**
- **Demonstrate a Life of Obedience**

I assume because you are working through this study, you already know to do—and probably successfully practice—some of these things. But I am guessing that, while you are familiar with the concepts, you have not yet fully understood or integrated the practice of one or more of them into your life. Even after all these years of studying this concept and walking closely with the Lord, I need to come back to these keys on a regular basis and reposition my heart and mind to hear God.

KEY #1: CULTIVATE A GROWING RELATIONSHIP WITH GOD

I love to meet people who work with my husband. I'm so proud of him. Everyone says nice things, from the top executive to the guy who mops the floor. I'm never surprised to hear them say he is helpful, honest, kind, attentive, and hard working. When people realize I'm Jon Cooper's wife, they gush—and I've come to expect the gushing. When they tell me what a great guy he is, I always say, "I know. He's like that at home, too."

If, upon introduction, a coworker said, "Yeah, nice to meet you. Your husband is a real jerk. He's completely unengaged from his employees. He's also lazy, mean, and manipulative," I'd laugh. Truly. Because anyone who would say such a thing would have to be joking. Or lying. Or mentally unstable.

See, I've known Jon since 1985—over 35 years now. I've spent a lot of time with him, talking to him, listening to him, watching him. I've seen him interact with his parents, his siblings, and his friends. I've observed him with all of our children at all different times of the day and night. We've worked through grief and marital problems. We've managed our home and finances together. I've taken the time to discover what he loves and what he hates, what makes him smile and what makes him sad. I've literally talked to him every day since the summer of 1992. I know Jon better than I know any other human. I know the sound of his voice. I recognize it immediately. I don't confuse Jon's voice with any other voice.

It wasn't always that way. In the days before cell phones and caller ID, when he first called my house and I answered the phone, he said, "Is Sandy there?" because he didn't recognize my voice. And I said, "This is Sandy speaking," and then waited for him to identify himself, because I didn't recognize his voice. And then we proceeded to have an awkward conversation, where I rambled and giggled a lot, because we didn't know each other yet, and we were also seventeen years old.

Jon has an identical twin brother named Joe. When we were young, Jon thought it was hilarious to put Joe on the phone and pretend it was Jon. You know how you can sense something is off, but you can't quite put your finger on it? Yeah, that was me every time they pulled this crap. When we first met, they fooled me every time, because I didn't know Jon. I knew some things about him, but I didn't *know* him. If Joe called me today and tried to imitate Jon, I would recognize it immediately. Not only does Joe's voice sound different than Jon's voice, but the words and phrases are different, too. They may be able to fool some people (and they often try this with nieces and nephews who don't see them together except once a year), but they can't fool me. Why? Because I know Jon—not just the sound of Jon's voice, but I know *Jon*.

"God's voice seems so faint to many Christians because they want the equivalent of a dating relationship with Him. But, He is looking for a marriage. A holy union. Oneness. He wants us to prioritize our relationship with him above all else."

Dr. Tony Evans.[12]

In the decades I've dedicated to studying this topic, I've discovered a direct correlation between *knowing* God and *hearing* God. In Lesson Two, we looked at numerous examples of God speaking to people in the Bible. The purpose of that lesson was to introduce some of the ways God has spoken and to illustrate the fact that God will speak to whomever He wants and however He wishes to achieve His sovereign plan.

But another theme woven all throughout Scripture is this: **The people who walked closely with the Lord heard His voice most clearly and most often.** The ones who loved God with their heart, mind, soul, and strength; the ones who loved God's law and obeyed Him; the ones who poured out their hearts to Him and inquired of Him—these were the people to whom God spoke freely and often. People like Noah and Abraham, Moses and Elijah, David and Daniel. The Bible shows us the practical ways these men walked closely with the Lord by praying to, inquiring of, and obeying the Living God. For the remainder of this lesson and into Lessons Four and Five, we will look at each of these men to help us understand how they lived and what God said to them.

Psalm 25:14 says,

The Lord confides in those who fear him; he makes his covenant known to them.

The word translated "confides" in that verse is the Hebrew word *sod*. *Sod* implies secrets, like those you'd share only with your best friend or your spouse. This is a verse taken from a Psalm of David—a man who could declare with confidence that God tells secrets to his closest friends. I want God to tell me secrets. Since you're working through this Bible study, maybe you want this, too. So, let's start with David and see what we can glean from his life that would help us become the people in whom God confides.

David

First, a giant disclaimer: One section of one lesson in one Bible study is not enough space to adequately study the life of David. In the Bible, we have opportunity to follow David through his entire life, beginning when he was a young shepherd boy, continuing throughout his reign as king, and ending with his death. His story spans four books of the Old Testament (**1 and 2 Samuel, 1 Kings, and 1 Chronicles**), and his name is mentioned 974 times in Scripture throughout the Old and New Testaments. Additionally, David penned 73 (and possibly as many as 85) of the 150 Psalms[13], giving us a rare and intimate look into his thoughts and prayers. We can read the events of David's life and then often read what David was thinking and praying *during those same events*! It's probably fair to say we know more about David that anyone else in the Bible, except for Jesus Christ. Our brief study will not do David justice, and I encourage you to read his entire story from beginning to end when you get a chance (See **Dig Deeper** at the end of this section).

David is one of the most notable men of all time for many reasons, not the least of which is his heart for God. One of the most familiar verses concerning David is found in **Acts 13:22**.

In your Bible look up **Acts 13:22**. What did God say about David in this verse?

_____

_____

_____

_____

Can you imagine a higher compliment from God, Himself? Yeah, me neither.

Let's dig around David's life and see what "a man after My own heart" does, exactly. Specifically, let's uncover some of the ways David demonstrated a close walk with the Lord. Then in Lesson Four we'll take a look at some examples of God speaking to David and note some interesting patterns that will reveal even more about David's actions and character traits.

We get our first glimpse of David in **1 Samuel 16**. God had just rejected Saul as king and sent the prophet Samuel to anoint someone to replace him. David was the youngest of Jesse's sons, and when Samuel arrived, David wasn't there—he was out tending sheep. We know David was young, handsome, and healthy-looking, but he didn't look like a king— at least not from the outside. In fact, Samuel would have anointed David's older brother Eliab, had God not warned him against it.

In your Bible read **I Samuel 16:7**. What does God see that humans don't see?

_____

REFLECT AND ASSESS

Have you ever been wrongfully judged or passed over because of your outward appearance? Explain.

_____

_____

_____

_____

The word translated "heart" in that verse is the Hebrew word *lebab*. It refers to the inner man—his mind and his will. It's the same word used in **Deuteronomy 6:4-9** below (emphasis mine)

*4 Hear, O Israel: The Lord our God, the Lord is one. 5 Love the Lord your God with all your **heart** and with all your soul and with all your strength. 6 These commandments that I give you today are to be on your **hearts**. 7 Impress them on your children. Talk about them when you sit at home and when you walk along the road, when you lie down and when you get up. 8 Tie them as symbols on your hands and bind them on your foreheads. 9 Write them on the doorframes of your houses and on your gates.*

In my study *Finding Your Balance*, we studied this passage at length. It is known as the *Shema*—the Jewish confession of faith recited daily by orthodox Jews and on every Sabbath day in the synagogue. What I just discovered is that *Shema* is the Hebrew word meaning *to hear*. (As a student of the Word, I always love to find these surprising connections.)

What was it about David's heart that afforded him such favor with God? Below, I've listed attributes and actions that reveal David's heart and distinguish David from his brothers, his peers, and all other kings. These are some of the ways David demonstrated a heart toward God and a cultivated a loving relationship with Him:

ATTRIBUTES	ACTIONS
Humble	Held his feet to God's path
Innocent	Did not associate with evil people
Generous	Obedient to God's word and law
Just	Faithful to serve others
Righteous	Found his strength in God
Repentant	Gave glory to God in his victories
Thankful	Put his faith in God
Worshipful	Kept his eyes on the Lord
	Taught others to love and serve the Lord
	Inquired of the Lord
	Defended the name of God, even in the face of death

Below I've selected several passages concerning David that show examples of one or more of these attributes and actions. **Choose two passages from each book of the Bible listed below and look them up in your Bible (for a total of 7 passages).** Then from the list above, choose the attributes or actions revealed about David's character in that passage (many passages have more than one action or attribute). In the "Notes" section, record any additional observations you make about David's life that are helpful to you in understanding his heart toward God. I've done one for you as an example.

1 SAMUEL

1 Sam 17:26	1 Sam 22:14 (I've done this one for you below)
1 Sam 17:34-37	1 Sam 23:16
1 Sam 18:18, 23	1 Sam 30:6
1 Sam 19:5	1 Sam 30: 21-30

EXAMPLE

Passage: I Sam 22:14

Attributes/Actions: Faithful to serve others

Notes: David's reputation for faithful service to others was obvious to those who knew him. When we have a heart toward God, people will notice.

Passage #1

Attributes/Actions: _____

Notes: _____

_____

_____

_____

Passage #2

Attributes/Actions: _____

Notes: _____

_____

_____

_____

_____

2 SAMUEL
2 Sam 6: 12-23
2 Sam 7: 18-29
2 Sam 8:15
2 Sam 9
2 Sam 12:13, 20

Passage #3
Attributes/Actions: _____

Notes: _____

_____

_____

_____

_____

_____

Passage #4
Attributes/Actions: _____

Notes: _____

_____

_____

_____

_____

_____

_____

1 KINGS
1 Kgs 2:1-4

Passage #5 I Kings 2:1-4:
Attributes/Actions: _____

Notes: _____

_____

_____

_____

_____

PSALMS

Ps 5:3	Ps 16:8	Ps 32:5
Ps 7:17	Ps 17:5	Ps 51 (as a whole)
Ps 8:3-5	Ps 22:20-24	Ps 51:17
Ps 9:1	Ps 25:15	Ps 56:12
Ps 13:5	Ps 26:4-5	Ps 59:16-17

Passage #6

Attributes/Actions: _____

Notes: _____

_____

_____

_____

_____

Passage #7

Attributes/Actions: _____

Notes: _____

_____

_____

_____

_____

_____

DIG DEEPER: Want to keep going? Look up the remaining passages listed and write the attributes and actions of David. Use a blank page in the back of the book or a page in your own journal to record your observations. For a more complete picture of David's character and his heart toward God, read the books of 1 Samuel and 2 Samuel in their entirety.

◀)) **Pause and Listen:** As you read through the passages you selected and worked through this exercise, did anything about David or his actions surprise you? Move you? Prompt you to examine your own heart?

_____

_____

_____

_____

_____

Consider how David's heart condition positioned him to hear God's voice. Record any conclusions you are drawing at this point in your study, even if they are fuzzy or incomplete:

_____

_____

_____

_____

_____

Do you have any questions for God? Ask them now:

_____

_____

_____

_____

_____

_____

✿

Daniel

Like David, Daniel was a young man whose love and devotion toward God not only afforded him favor with kings, but also allowed him to hear God's voice clearly and often.

In 605 BC, King Nebuchadnezzar besieged Jerusalem, forcing Daniel and his friends, along with other captives of the Judean nobility, to come to Babylon. The king intended to teach them the language and literature of the Babylonians over the course of three years and then use them for the king's service. So, he chose the best young men he could find—strong, handsome, and intelligent. He stripped them of their Hebrew names and culture, and set before them daily food and wine from the king's table.

So far in the story, we know that Daniel was extremely attractive, well-informed, and quick to understand. But his response to his new diet is what gives us the first glimpse into Daniel's love for God.

Daniel 1:8

8 But Daniel resolved not to defile himself with the royal food and wine, and he asked the chief official for permission not to defile himself this way.

Daniel was probably only about 15 years old at the time. Yet, even at this young age, Daniel demonstrated devotion to God and His law. See, this was not just food and wine to Daniel. The royal diet consisted of non-kosher meat—probably pork and horseflesh—as well as alcohol offered to the Babylonian gods. Daniel had set in his heart that he did not want to defile himself with foods and practices, which were strictly forbidden by the Jewish Law. Therefore, he asked for permission to abstain from the royal diet—a very risky, and potentially deadly request. In return for their faithfulness and devotion, God richly rewarded Daniel and his friends.

> In your Bible, read **Daniel 1:17**. How did God reward them?
>
> _____
>
> _____

Some time later (probably about three years—the time allotted for Daniel's training), King Nebuchadnezzar suffered through a series of disturbing dreams. So, the king sought out wise men and counselors to help him understand them. Except he asked for the impossible: he wanted the wise men to not only interpret the dreams, but also *reveal the content of the dreams*. In other words, he said, "Tell me what my dream means. But first, tell me what my dream *was*." The counselors insisted that this sort of request was outrageous—what man on earth could possibly interpret the dream *and tell the king exactly what he dreamed*? Nebuchadnezzar was resolute: failure to meet the king's conditions would bring death to all the royal counselors, including Daniel and his friends (who, as far as we can tell, had not even been consulted on the matter).

When Daniel learned of the king's decree, he boldly approached the king and asked for time so that he may interpret it according the king's unbelievable specifications. And this is where we get another glimpse into Daniel's relationship with the Lord.

In your Bible, read **Daniel 2:17-23**. What did Daniel do next? What do his actions reveal about His walk with the Lord?

_____

_____

_____

_____

_____

_____

Then, a few chapters later (**Daniel 5**), we read a very strange story. Years had passed, Nebuchadnezzar was dead, and Belshazzar was the new king. One night, King Belshazzar decided to throw a giant party for a thousand of his friends, their wives, and their concubines. While feasting, he gave orders to bring out the gold and silver vessels, which had been taken from the Jewish temple during the siege. Then he and his guests drank wine from the vessels while they praised the gods of gold and silver, of bronze, iron, wood, and stone.

This is where we shake our heads and say, "Oh no they didn't."

Yes. Yes, they did. Their behavior was an aggressive and blasphemous act toward the God of Israel, to say the least. Using the holy vessels was bad enough, but worshipping false gods *while using the holy vessels?!* Stupid. So very stupid.

At that precise moment when the king and his nobles mocked the One True God, the finger of a man's hand emerged and began writing on a plaster wall. They all freaked out (as you can imagine) and then called for Daniel to interpret the writing.

In your Bible, read **Daniel 5:16-17**. What did the king promise Daniel for his interpretation?

_____

_____

How did Daniel respond to the king's offer?

_____

_____

Why do you think Daniel responded so boldly?

_____

_____

Then, Daniel basically told the king, "Your actions and attitude are appalling, and—oh, by the way—the God whom you mock holds your life in His hands. The writing on the wall says that you're gonna die. Buh-bye." (Obviously, paraphrased.)

That very night, Belshazzar died; proving Daniel's interpretation true, and Darius became king.

By this time, we see that Daniel was a man of such outstanding character and possessed favor with both God and people that the king decided to set him over the entire kingdom. This made the other rulers and administrators serving under King Darius extremely jealous. They tried to find grounds for charges against Daniel in his conduct of government affairs, but they were unable to do so. The Bible says, "they could find no corruption in him, because he was trustworthy and neither corrupt nor negligent."

In your Bible read **Daniel 6:5**. What was Daniel's only "fault" according to the Babylonian rulers?

_____

_____

So, the rulers convinced the king to issue a decree stating that anyone who prayed to any god or man, besides to the king himself, would be thrown into the lions' den.

In your Bible read Daniel **6:10-11**. What did Daniel do when he learned of the decree?

_____

_____

In case you don't know how this story ends, the jealous men caught Daniel praying, as they knew they would, and reported back to the king. The king was devastated because he really liked Daniel. But since he had signed the irrevocable law, his hands were tied. The king reluctantly gave the order, and the men threw Daniel into the lions' den. Meanwhile, the king went back to his palace and stayed up all night grieving and fasting for Daniel. In the morning, the king hurried back to the lions' den to see Daniel's fate, only to find Daniel alive! God had sent an angel to close the mouths of the lions. Then the king ordered the men who had falsely accused Daniel, along with their wives and children, to be thrown into the lions' den instead. They were dead within minutes. King Darius issued a new decree stating that the God of Daniel is the Living God, and Daniel continued to prosper during the remainder of Darius' reign and the reign of Cyrus the Persian. He also continued to hear God speak through visions and dreams.

 DIG DEEPER: Read Daniel 7-12 to see how God continued to speak to Daniel.

SUMMARY

- Daniel was devoted to God and to His law, even in the face of punishment.

- In time of crisis, Daniel sought God and encouraged his friends to do the same.

- Daniel believed that God would speak to him.

- When God spoke to Daniel, he gave all the glory to God.

- Daniel was not motivated by external rewards but by his love for God.

- Daniel was a man of prayer.

- Daniel honored God by doing excellent work, even though he was technically a captive and a slave in a pagan city.

Would you add anything to this summary?

_____

_____

_____

_____

One of the most powerful and effective methods to learn how to position ourselves to hear God's voice is by studying the lives of the people in the Bible to whom God spoke most often. In the lives of David and Daniel, we see that the secret to their "hearing ability" was their depth of love toward God—despite unfathomable opposition. Beginning at a young age and continuing all throughout their lives, these men demonstrated unshakable faith and intimate communion with the Lord. These are our examples. If we want to be good listeners, we can learn to walk as they walked.

◀)) **Pause and Listen:** Ask God what He wants you to do with what you just learned about David and Daniel. Is God showing you an area of your heart that needs to change? Is He showing you a tangible way you can walk more closely with Him? Is God showing you areas of your heart He's especially pleased with—practices and habits that are already strong and effective? (I bet you are already doing so many good things to foster this relationship with Him!) Ask Him right now to speak to you. Then pause and listen. Write down what you think God is saying:

_____

_____

_____

_____

_____

_____

_____

_____

_____

_____

KEY #2: SATURATE YOUR MIND WITH SCRIPTURE

I was at the grocery store when I spotted an acquaintance from church. I said hello, gave her a quick hug, and asked her how she was doing. Rather than the typical, "fine thanks, how are you?" she proceeded to tell me how she was *actually doing.*

Recently divorced, she was struggling to balance her time between her young children and her full-time work—work that she dreaded with a company she hated. She was navigating a complicated shared-custody agreement with her ex-husband. She was feeling lonely and isolated in church, where it appeared to her that everyone was happily married, except for her. And, on top of all that, she had ongoing conflicts with her adult siblings over the care of their aging parents.

Whoa. To say that I was outside my skill set and realm of experience would be an understatement. I had no idea how to advise this hurting woman who had just spilled her guts to me in the middle of the produce section. So, I hugged her again, and told her I was sorry for everything she was dealing with. And then I asked her, "What is God saying to you right now?"

She said, "I don't hear God's voice at all. I don't think He speaks to me."

"Hmmm. Well, God will always speak to you through the Bible. How often are you in the Word of God?"

She narrowed her eyes as she carefully considered her response. Then shook her head, "Never. Outside of church, I don't read the Bible at all."

Part declaration. Part confession.

"Well, friend," I said, "I won't pretend to know what God will say to you, but I know that spending time in His word is a good place to start if you want to hear Him say something."

In your Bible, find the following verses and write them out word-for-word

2 Timothy 3:14-17:

_____

_____

_____

_____

2 Peter 1:20-21:

_____

_____

_____

_____

Hebrews 4:12:

_____

_____

_____

_____

The Bible, quite literally, is God's voice in written form. So, the second key to becoming a good listener is to immerse yourself in the Bible.

REFLECT AND ASSESS

Before we go any further, let me ask you the same question I asked my friend: How much time are you currently spending in the word of God? Consider all forms (reading, listening, etc.). If it's not often, don't be ashamed. Instead, let this serve as a starting point from which you can launch and grow:

_____

_____

_____

_____

_____

_____

God's primary way of speaking to us is through His written word. God has already spoken in the Bible about every issue for which we seek clarity and guidance—if not specifically, then in principle. For example, the Bible will not tell you specifically where to set boundaries for technology-use in your home, but it will tell you to guard your heart (**Prov 4:23**), to honor God in everything you do (**Col 3:17**), to ask God for wisdom (**Jas 1:5**), to take every thought captive and make it obedient to Christ (**2 Cor 10:5**), and to refrain from having idols (**I Jn 5:21**). By obeying the words and laws God has already established, we can often discern direction and clarity for specific situations.

Most of the time when God speaks to me, it is when I'm already reading, meditating on, or studying Scripture. Other times, God will bring a passage back to my mind that I had read or heard previously. Spending time in God's word gives us regular opportunity to hear His words and provides a "library of truths" for Him to work with to impress instruction or guidance on our hearts when we are not actively reading the Bible.

When a Christian—including myself—struggles to recognize God's voice or fails to hear Him speak at all, it is usually because he or she is not actively engaging with God's word on a regular basis. (Exceptions to this exist, as we will discuss in a minute.) I cannot overstate this. There is a direct correlation between the amount of time a person spends reading and studying the Bible and that person's ability to hear God's voice. So, if you are having a difficult time hearing God speak, your first and second priorities are these:

❋   To pursue a genuine relationship with God

❋   To become intentional about consuming His word daily

These keys tie for first place in significance. They go hand-in-hand and cannot be separated. You cannot know God without reading His word and you cannot understand His word without seeking a genuine relationship with Him.

Read **John 5:36-40** below and answer the question that follows:

"**36** I have testimony weightier than that of John. For the works that the Father has given me to finish—the very works that I am doing—testify that the Father has sent me. **37** And the Father who sent me has himself testified concerning me. You have never heard his voice nor seen his form, **38** nor does his word dwell in you, for you do not believe the one he sent. **39** You study the Scriptures diligently because you think that in them you have eternal life. These are the very Scriptures that testify about me, **40** yet you refuse to come to me to have life."

The person speaking here is Jesus. He's addressing the Jewish leaders who were plotting his death because He had just healed a paralytic on the Sabbath, and He also claimed to be "equal with God." (See **John 5:1-35**) These Jewish leaders were meticulous about studying Scripture. They were known for it. Took pride in it. Boasted and bragged about it, even. But despite their diligent study, they couldn't hear God's voice. In fact, they managed to miss the whole point—the very heart of the Scriptures they studied!

> Look carefully at verses 38 and 40. Why was this? Why couldn't they hear God's voice?
>
> _____
>
> _____
>
> _____

So, while it is imperative that we dedicate our lives to the study of God's word, hear me: It is possible to have a doctorate in theology, have a reputation for meticulous study of God's word, and still not hear the voice of God. It is possible to work through Bible study after Bible study, month after month, and still miss the whole point and heart of Scripture. Head knowledge and heart transformation are not the same thing. We can't *only* study the Scriptures. We must also believe that Jesus is the Son of God and we must seek Him for eternal life.

"Scripture is the primary way God speaks. It is not only the main way you will hear Him, but it also provides the boundaries into which everything else He says to you will fall. If you ignore this chief means of divine communication, you will never hear God clearly."

Priscilla Shirer[14]

Also, God's voice will never contradict His written word. If you are hearing something that directly contradicts a truth found in Scripture, you can be 100% sure that *it is not God.* In fact, I like to say that God's voice sounds exactly like His word. So, the more we familiarize ourselves with the Bible, the more we learn the language of God. We learn about God's character, His motives, and His methods of communication. We learn what He loves and what He hates. We learn what He embraces and resists. Then, when we have a thought and wonder, is *the voice in my head God, or just me,* we can often answer that question by simply comparing the voice in our head to the voice of God in Scripture.

One of the most common ways I see this play out in the lives of women is in the thoughts we have about ourselves. *I'm lazy. I'm selfish. I'm stupid.* Never in Scripture do we see God address His children as lazy, selfish, or stupid. He often confronts our sin, but He never calls us names. Also, since *God is love* and everything He does is rooted in love for us, when we hear a voice rooted in condemnation, self-deprecation, or hate, we can know—without a doubt—this is not God's voice, because it doesn't sound anything like the voice of God we see in Scripture. This is why we must continually run our thoughts and impressions through the filter of God's word.

So, if we want to incline our ear to hear—if we want to arrange our lives in such a way as to make hearing possible—we must learn God's word, know God's word, and absorb God's word. We can't accomplish this by simply dipping our toe into it. We must have a headfirst, all-in, full-immersion attitude.

REFLECT AND ASSESS

When you read, "We must have a head-first, all-in, full-immersion attitude," what is your initial reaction to this? Check the phrase that best describes your thinking.

☐ **I know this and try to live this way**

☐ **I know this but don't live this way**

☐ **I suspected this but wasn't sure**

☐ **This is news to me**

☐ **Other:** _____

Let's take a look at some practical ways to put this *full-immersion attitude* into practice.

A. Bible Reading

Bible reading is exactly what it implies—simply reading the Scriptures. We do this to acquire knowledge, but we also do it for the purpose of spiritual nourishment.

Matthew chapter 4 tells of the story of the temptation of Jesus. It says that after Jesus had fasted 40 days and 40 nights, He was hungry. So, Satan came to Him and tempted Him with food—bread to be exact. *Tell these stones to become bread* he said. Can you think of anything more tempting than a loaf of fresh, warm, crusty bread when you're hungry? Or not hungry? Me neither.

Jesus' response to Satan is one of the most often-quoted verses in Scripture. In your Bible find **Matthew 4:4** and write it here, word-for-word:

_____

_____

_____

Jesus was quoting **Deuteronomy 8:3** where Moses was preparing the Children of Israel to enter the Promised Land. He reminded them that God provided manna for them to eat in the wilderness to show them *that they must rely on God and His word for spiritual nourishment—even in the Promised Land.*

This idiom of spiritual food implies more than just reading, of course. It also means digesting it and allowing it to become part of you for the purpose of growth and strength. We see this idiom throughout Scripture. Let's look at one more found in **I Peter 1:22-2:3** (NASB, emphasis mine):

"**22** *Since you have in obedience to the truth purified your souls for a sincere love of the brethren, fervently love one another from the heart,* **23** *for you have been born again not of seed which is perishable but imperishable, that is, through* **the living and enduring word of God**. **24** *For,*

"*All flesh is like grass,*
And all its glory like the flower of grass.
The grass withers,
And the flower falls off,

25 But **the word of the Lord** *endures forever."*

And this is **the word which was preached to you**.

2 Therefore, putting aside all malice and all deceit and hypocrisy and envy and all slander, **2 like newborn babies, long for the pure milk of the word,** *so that by it you may grow in respect to salvation, 3 if you have tasted the kindness of the Lord."*

The word translated "pure" in **I Peter 2:2** refers to food that is unadulterated, not mixed with anything else—like breast milk for infants. Peter is telling us to crave the word the way newborns crave breast milk. Have you ever been around a newborn? Have you have *fed* a newborn?

They eat all day and all night.

Every three to four hours.

'Round the clock.

Every day.

And every night.

Day after day after day.

(I feel sleep-deprived just typing that.)

An adult can survive weeks, even months, without food. But newborns? They will die within days if they don't eat. **This is how God wants us to approach His word. Like you will die if you don't have it.**

If you already do this—read the Bible daily for the purpose of spiritual nourishment—feel free to skip over this section. But if all this is new to you or you have not yet made this a daily practice, allow me to make a few suggestions to help you approach the Bible this way. These are not set in stone and this is not the only way. So, if it's helpful to you, awesome. Otherwise, do what works best for you to create a life where Bible reading is a daily habit and part of your spiritual disciplines.

First, it is common for people intending to read the Bible to start at the beginning in Genesis and try to read all the way through to Revelation.

It sounds reasonable, since this is how we approach most books—start at the beginning and read to the end. I don't recommend this with approaching Scripture. If you're like me, you'll start out strong in Genesis and Exodus (the stories really are fascinating!) but get bogged down somewhere in Leviticus or Numbers with all the census-taking and Law-giving.

This is because not all of God's word is "milk." Some of it is "meat." That means it is difficult to digest if you are a baby (a new believer) in Christ. In fact, if you tried to shove a piece of steak into a newborn's mouth, you would choke her. Other parts of the Bible are a lot like exotic fruit and bitter herbs and hot chili peppers. These parts require some serious explanation and/or spiritual revelation (which we will talk about in a minute). So, if you are just starting out or struggle to stay engaged, and you want to find practical ways to read God's word for daily nourishment, here are a few tips.

Bible Reading Tips to Maximize Understanding and Avoid Fizzling Out

- Start in the Gospel of John. This book was written by one of Jesus' closest friends for the purpose of showing Jesus' divinity.

- After John, read through the other three Gospels (Matthew, Mark, and Luke.). These also tell the story of Jesus, but from different perspectives.

- Next, read the Book of Acts, which tells about birth of the early Church.

- Then read through the Epistles (Romans, 1 and 2 Corinthians, Galatians, Ephesians, Philippians, Colossians, 1 and 2 Thessalonians, 1 and 2 Timothy, Titus, Philemon, Hebrews, James, 1 and 2 Peter, 1, 2 and 3 John, and Jude), which are the letters to the Church that discuss how to live a life devoted to Christ.

- Skip Revelation for now—it can be very confusing because it's a description of a prophetic vision and full of imagery and symbolism.

- Now, go all the way back to the beginning of the Bible and read Genesis and Exodus. This tells the story of creation, as well as the stories of pivotal Old Testament characters like Noah, Moses, Joseph, Abraham, Isaac, and Jacob. It also tells about the beginning of the nation of Israel, God's chosen people.

- Next read through Psalms and Proverbs.

- At this point, you can either start over again, or tackle some of the other Old Testament books and Revelation.

- Treat this as your daily spiritual nourishment, just like you would a meal.

- Read whenever you can, preferably in the morning, and all throughout the day.

- When a verse jumps off the page, underline it or write it down, and meditate on it (see below)

- Take your time. Many Bible reading plans lead you through the entire Bible in a year. But I have found that slower, more thoughtful reading is much more conducive to hearing God's voice, and less like a checklist to complete. As Henry Blackaby says, we shouldn't just read God's word so that it passes through our minds like water though a pipe.[15]

REFLECT AND ASSESS If you have an established habit of daily Bible reading, what is working well for you? What could you improve to maximize your understanding and satisfaction while you consume God's word?

_____

_____

_____

_____

If you do not have an established habit of daily Bible reading, why is that? Have you attempted and got stuck? If it didn't go as well as you hoped, what derailed you?

_____

_____

_____

_____

_____

What plan can you put into place right now that will help you overcome that obstacle?

A
P
P   _____
L
Y   _____

_____

_____

B. Biblical Meditation

Sometimes we eat food simply because we are hungry—out of complete necessity. There is absolutely nothing wrong with this. And other times we savor our meal. We take our time. We note the texture and the aroma and the beauty of the dish. We enjoy each morsel as we slowly and intentionally bite... chew... swallow. Dallas Willard said, "It is better in one year to have ten good verses transferred into the substance of our lives than to have every word of the Bible flash before our eyes."[16] This practice of _transferring verses into the substance of our lives_ is known as Biblical meditation.

Though some similarities exist, Biblical meditation is not to be confused with meditation associated with Eastern religions. Like Eastern meditation, Biblical meditation involves emptying our mind of all wrong thinking. But unlike Eastern meditation, Biblical meditation means replacing those thoughts with God's promises and attributes found in His word. Biblical meditation is an act of discipline whereby we hold a truth of God's word in our heart and mind and let it marinate. Sometimes, it means simply dwelling on one verse or one scriptural principle for a day or a week or longer.

The Bible speaks of meditation often, especially in the book of Psalms. Read **Psalm 77:1-12** below. Circle every word or phrase that implies meditation (Hint: also look for words like "thought," "remember," etc.)

Psalm 77

"**1** I cried out to God for help; I cried out to God to hear me. **2** When I was in distress, I sought the Lord; at night I stretched out untiring hands, and I would not be comforted. **3** I remembered you, God, and I groaned; I meditated, and my spirit grew faint. **4** You kept my eyes from closing; I was too troubled to speak.

5 I thought about the former days, the years of long ago; **6** I remembered my songs in the night. My heart meditated and my spirit asked: **7** 'Will the Lord reject forever? Will he never show his favor again? **8** Has his unfailing love vanished forever? Has his promise failed for all time? **9** Has God forgotten to be merciful? Has he in anger withheld his compassion?'

10 Then I thought, 'To this I will appeal: the years when the Most High stretched out his right hand. **11** I will remember the deeds of the Lord; yes, I will remember your miracles of long ago. **12** I will consider all your works and meditate on all your mighty deeds.'"

Below are several short verses that specifically mention meditation. Choose any three from the list below and write them out word-for-word in the space provided:

Psalm 19:14   **Psalm 119:15**   **Psalm 119:48**

Psalm 49:3   **Psalm 119:23**   **Psalm 119:78**

Psalm 104:34   **Psalm 119:27**   **Psalm 119:148**

1. _____

_____

_____

_____

2. _____

_____

_____

_____

3. _____

_____

_____

_____

 DIG DEEPER: Want to keep going? Read the rest of the verses about meditation listed above, recording any thoughts you have as you go.

Besides the ability to discern the voice of God more clearly, Biblical meditation has many other benefits as well.

In your Bible, look up the following verses, and then write the benefit of meditating on God's word mentioned there.

1. Joshua 1:8

_____

2. Psalm 1:1-4

_____

3. Psalm 119:97-98

_____

4. Psalm 119:99

_____

If you have never intentionally sought to develop a daily habit of Biblical meditation, here are a few ways to approach it that work well for me.

Practical ways to Meditate on Scripture

- Whenever you are reading Scripture or listening to a sermon and a passage jumps out at you, write it down. I like to write these verses either in my journal or on index cards.

- Post the passage in a place where you will see it every day (on your mirror, on your dash board, over your kitchen sink, as the wallpaper on your phone, etc.)

- Look up the verse in several Bible translations to get a full understanding of the meaning. I especially like using _The Amplified Bible_ for this purpose. I also suggest using an online tool like _Biblegateway.com_ for this, where you have access to dozens of translations.

- ❊ Commit the passage to memory.

- ❊ Spend 30 full minutes reading and re-reading the passage. Write down every thought or insight you have about the passage. You'll probably find your best insights come towards the end of this timeframe.

- ❊ Choose a chapter or a shorter book of the Bible that is especially meaningful to you and read it every day for a week or a month. Every time you read it you'll find new portions jumping out at you. Write down your thoughts. If you like to write in your Bible, circle words, underline sentences, and write in the margins.

- ❊ Listen to and sing with music that uses Scripture in the lyrics.

- ❊ Incorporate Scripture into prayer. Some passages are already in prayer form, like the Psalms. But other passages can be reworked and prayed back to God. I like to write out prayers for specific needs using Scripture (a prayer for peace, a prayer for wisdom, a prayer for my children, etc.) I write these out in my journal and pray them in the morning.

Biblical meditation is probably the most effective means of turning off the other voices in your head. It allows the Holy Spirit to speak quietly and clearly into the depths of your spirit and unfold layer after layer of a truth or promise. When you begin this meditative practice, you'll start to notice God confirming His voice to you by speaking the same scripture repeatedly, through a song, through a sermon, through a book, or through a friend.

John Ortberg said, "What repeatedly enters your mind and occupies your mind eventually shapes your mind and will ultimately express itself in what you do and who you become."[17] If you want to be a person who knows how to hear God's voice, then allow your mind to be occupied, completely, repeatedly, with God's word.

C. Bible Study

My husband and I have been moving toward a plant-based diet for the last couple years, so I'm often looking for something new to make for dinner that doesn't involve meat or dairy (more food analogies!). Have you ever been looking at a new recipe you're excited to try, only to read through the ingredients list and find something you never heard of? Yeah, that's me and *nutritional yeast*. (Bread aisle? Baking aisle? Vitamin Shoppe?) Also, *coconut aminos*. (Is this sold in a test tube?) Or maybe you recognize the ingredient, but you have never cooked with it and, therefore, have no earthly clue how to handle it. (I'm looking at you, tofu...*silken, soft, medium, firm, extra firm, super firm*. Is this food or a mattress?)

Sometimes it's exactly like that with God's word. Some parts of the Bible are easy to understand, easy to consume, easy to digest. We know exactly what to do with *love is patient, love is kind,* for example, because this is the milk of God's word.

But often when we are reading Scripture, we come across something unusual, strange, or outright disturbing (I'm still looking at you, *tofu!*) Maybe it's something we thought we understood—with our English translation, in the context of our Western culture, in the year 2000-something— but the author intended it to mean something completely different.

After all, the Bible is a collection of 66 books written in three different languages, by 40 different authors from all over the Middle East, over the span of 1,500 years. The literary genres include law, history, poetry, prophecy, and letters. To attempt to handle God's word without some knowledge of what we are reading is ineffective and can be misleading or dangerous.

This is why we must not only read scripture and meditate on Scripture, but we must also study it.

Read Ezra 7:8-10 (CSB) below and answer the question that follows.

"**8** *Ezra came to Jerusalem in the fifth month, during the seventh year of the king.* **9** *He began the journey from Babylon on the first day of the first* *month and arrived in Jerusalem on the first day of the fifth month since the gracious hand of his God was on him.* **10** *Now Ezra had determined in his heart to study the law of the Lord, obey it, and teach its statutes and ordinances in Israel."*

> This passage says that the "gracious hand of his God" was on Ezra because Ezra did three things. What was Ezra determined to do? Go back and underline them. (v. 10)

Not all reading of Scripture is a *study* of Scripture. A Bible study is where we do a combination of the following:

❀ Read passages in context or a book of the Bible as a whole unit

❀ Identify the author and the intended audience of the book

❀ Look at the original language or multiple translations to help with difficult passages

❀ Look at the culture to understand references and metaphors

❀ Examine related scriptures

This is exactly what you are doing right now in this study. (Yay you!)

2 Timothy 2:15 says to *"Do your best to present yourself to God as one approved, a worker who does not need to be ashamed and who correctly handles the word of truth."* The King James Version translates the phrase "do your best" as "study." Both phrases imply a diligence and persistence to understand and impart the word of God completely, accurately, and clearly. **Study, so that you can correctly handle God's word.**

You can do all this on your own with the help of Bible study tools like commentaries, Bible dictionaries, and study Bibles (like I'm doing now as I write this), or you can follow someone else's study who has done the work for you (like you are doing now as you work through this).

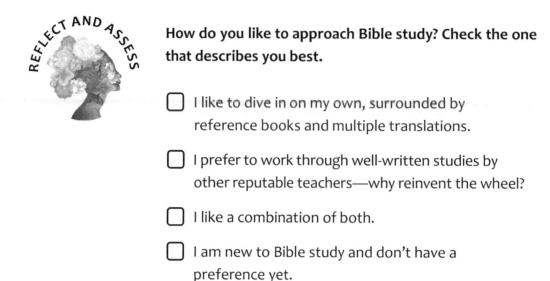

How do you like to approach Bible study? Check the one that describes you best.

☐ I like to dive in on my own, surrounded by reference books and multiple translations.

☐ I prefer to work through well-written studies by other reputable teachers—why reinvent the wheel?

☐ I like a combination of both.

☐ I am new to Bible study and don't have a preference yet.

There are benefits to both approaches—I do one or the other, depending on what I'm studying. For example, as I write this, my dining room table is strewn with books and notes and Bibles, and I have four open tabs on my computer for websites I continually reference as I work through the Scriptures. But, later tonight, I'll attend a weekly line-by-line study of the books of Ruth and Esther at my church. The Ruth and Esther study is not part of my preparation for this book, but just another way for me to grow in my faith and learn God's word. The teacher of the Ruth and Esther study has taken the time to study those books in great detail, and I'm benefiting from her months of preparation, the same way you are benefitting from my months (years!) of preparation now as you work through this study.

If you are new to Bible study, this all can sound very intimidating, right? So, hear me when I say this: **the word of God is accessible to you!** In fact, the accessibility that we currently enjoy (especially as women!) is unprecedented in the history of the world. Never before have we had so many translations, commentaries, maps, dictionaries, and websites—not to mention, seminaries and Bible schools—at our fingertips to help us handle the word of God correctly. But you don't need to run out and purchase a library of commentaries or obtain a degree in theology in order to handle God's word responsibly. God has given the gift of teaching to many people within the Church. You can work through a Bible study in the privacy of your home or in a group. That means all the legwork is done for you, and it is written or presented to you in an easily digestible format.

Now, if you love the idea of building up your commentary library and digging in yourself, by all means, go for it. I would be honored to sit down to work through *your* study some day!

SUMMARY

- Inclining your ear to hear means to stretch, reach, and arrange your life in such a way as to make hearing God possible.

- The first key to becoming a good listener is to Cultivate a Growing Relationship with God.

- By studying the lives of people to whom God spoke on a regular basis—like David and Daniel—we can learn how they cultivated an intimate relationship with Him and incorporate these habits and actions into our own lives.

- The second key to becoming a good listener is to Saturate Your Mind With Scripture, through Bible reading, Biblical meditation, and Bible study.

- These keys tie for first place in significance. They go hand-in-hand and cannot be separated. You cannot know God without reading His word and you cannot understand His word without seeking a genuine relationship with Him.

FOR DISCUSSION

* Can you think of a time God spoke clearly and directly to you through His Word? What did He say?

_____

_____

_____

_____

_____

_____

_____

_____

_____

_____

_____

_____

_____

_____

_____

_____

_____

❀   We are blessed to live in a time when we have access to the word of God in many other forms besides a leather-bound book. What are some other ways you can consume God's word that are not just reading or studying the Bible? Think outside the box.

_____

_____

_____

_____

_____

_____

_____

_____

_____

_____

_____

_____

_____

_____

_____

_____

_____

_____

❋   What you fill your mind with outside of Bible reading or Bible study is also important. In fact, this will affect how you hear God within your Bible study/Bible reading time. In the same way my literal food affects my strength and endurance in my workouts, what I consume in my mind affects me when I try to do the work God has set before me. Discuss how our choices of entertainment, friendships, hobbies, etc., can affect our ability to hear God.

_____

_____

_____

_____

_____

_____

_____

_____

_____

_____

_____

_____

_____

_____

_____

❀ What is your biggest take-away from this lesson?

_____

_____

_____

_____

_____

_____

_____

_____

_____

_____

_____

_____

_____

_____

_____

_____

_____

_____

_____

_____

Lesson Four

The 5 Keys to Becoming a Good Listener (cont.)

INTEGRATE PERIODS OF SOLITUDE
EMULATE A SPIRIT OF HUMILITY

"Here's what I want you to do: Find a quiet, secluded place so you won't be tempted to role-play before God. Just be there as simply and honestly as you can manage. The focus will shift from you to God, and you will begin to sense his grace."

MATTHEW 6:6 (MSG)

A study published in 2002 in *Psychological Science* examined the effects that airport noise had on children's health and cognition. The study revealed that children exposed to noise develop a stress response, which causes them to ignore the noise. That sounds like a good thing, right? Except, these children not only ignore the harmful airport noise, but also all helpful stimuli, as well—even speech.

According to Gary W. Evans, a professor of human ecology at Cornell University, "This study is among the strongest, probably the most definitive proof, that noise – even at levels that do not produce any hearing damage – causes stress and is harmful to humans."

Extensive studies on the effects of noise show that noise harms task performance at both work and school. It decreases motivation and increases errors. It affects reading comprehension, memory, and problem solving. Children exposed to excessive noise suffer lower reading scores and are slower in their development of cognitive and language skills.

But, here's the good news: *Silence appears to have the opposite effect.* In as little as two minutes of silence, we experience positive changes in blood pressure and blood circulation to the brain. In silence, the brain is able to let down its sensory guard and restore some of what has been 'lost' through excess noise.[18]

What is true about literal noise is also true for spiritual noise. We have never lived in a "louder" time in the history of the world. To be fair, we don't all live near airports, but we are all bombarded with incessant noise, both internally and externally.

Consider the average American spends over three hours a day on a mobile device. A third of us say we are online "almost constantly,"[19] where we see anywhere from 4,000 to 10,000 ads per day. We have television streaming 24 hours per day, while also holding our hand-held devices, scrolling, scrolling, scrolling. When we drive, we flip on the radio or resume a podcast or make phone calls. When we walk, we pop in our earbuds and listen to an audiobook. We do housework to the sound of our playlist. We fall asleep to the hum of the television. We wake to the sound of the radio.

One study suggests the average person gets a mere 63 minutes a day of complete silence.[20] I don't know about you, but that estimate sounds high to me.

REFLECT AND ASSESS

How much time a day do you think you have complete silence?

☐ **Silence? What's that?**

☐ **Less than an hour**

☐ **About an hour**

☐ **Two hours or more**

Not all noise is bad noise. I love podcasts and music. Audiobooks are a wonderful convenience for book-lovers like me. I like HGTV as much as the next gal. **But is it any wonder—with multiple streams of stimuli flooding our minds perpetually—that we have a difficult time hearing God's voice?** In order to hear God better, we must learn to make room for Him in our thoughts.

Psalm 10:4 says, *"In his pride the wicked man does not seek him;* **in all his thoughts there is no room for God."** (Emphasis mine)

A quick review: in Lesson Three we introduced **The 5 Keys to Becoming a Good Listener** and studied Key #1 and Key #2. Before we introduce Key #3, do you remember what they were?

* Cultivate _____

* Saturate _____

* Integrate Periods of Solitude

* Emulate a Spirit of Humility

* Demonstrate a Life of Obedience

❀

Key #3: Integrate Periods of Solitude

*"For certain, there has not been enough silence in my life.
Silence is the condition for true listening. But I have too little of it.
Silence came visiting and found me already occupied. The element of
silence for me is scanty and thin. My existence is a welter of noise."*
Mark Buchanan[21]

Maybe the thought of slipping away alone for the sole purpose of being silent sounds self-indulgent to you. Maybe you feel guilty for even considering taking time away from your job, your children, or other responsibilities. Maybe you don't feel like you deserve time alone. I can relate to this. When my kids were very little and I was home with them all-day-every-day, rarely did I feel like I "deserved" time alone.

After all, I chose to have these children. I chose to set aside my career in order to be home with them. To actively seek time to flee their presence tipped toward "unloving." It wasn't their fault they were noisy. And messy. (The messy part isn't relevant to this conversation, but I just feel the need to justify the fact that my house was trashed for the better part of two decades, despite my constant cleaning.)

Instead of acknowledging that need for silence, I'd suppress it. I'd tell myself, *you're fine... Suck it up.* I'd picture the teary-eyed older women in Target (who'd always stop me while I was trying to navigate the cart through the narrow aisles while kids hung onto the edges, making it impossible to steer) reminding me to enjoy every moment—even the noisy ones. Which, incidentally, were *all the moments.*

The suppression strategy always worked...right up until I'd snap, after which, I'd find myself crouched on the floor behind the laundry room door, crying hot wet tears because *CAN I JUST HAVE FIVE MINUTES OF QUIET PLEASE?!* Or Jon would walk in after a 10-hour workday, and I'd abruptly hand him a sticky toddler in the doorway, then peel out of the driveway like I was late for my appointment with *SILENCE.*

This *suck-it-up-until-you-snap* strategy is not conducive to hearing God.

Then I discovered all the times in the Bible where Jesus broke away from the crowds to be alone. Think about that. Jesus—as in, God in the flesh—intentionally walked away from people (!) in order to be alone.

In your Bible, find **Luke 5:16** and write it here word-for-word:

_____

_____

_____

If Jesus needed solitude, then who am I to think I don't?

Below are six examples recorded in Scripture where Jesus chose solitude, each for a different situation. In your Bible, look up the following passages. Then draw a line matching the example to one of the situations listed.

Passage	Situation Where Jesus Chose Solitude
Mark 1:16-35	Before He launched His public ministry
Matthew 14:1-13	Before He chose His twelve disciples
Matthew 14:14-23	After a full day and night of ministry to people
Matthew 4:1-17	To focus on prayer
Matthew 26:36-46	To grieve
Luke 6:12-16	To strengthen Himself when He knew He was about to suffer and die.

By the way, did you notice in the passages how many times people came searching for Jesus when He tried to be alone? Does this sound like your life? Yeah, mine too! To be sure, solitude won't come easily. If we do not intentionally carve out times of silence and solitude, and guard them with our lives, we will never have it.

Can you recall a time recently when you tried to be alone or have silence and people interrupted you? What happened? How did you respond?

_____

_____

_____

Not only did Jesus model solitude, but also He instructed his disciples to do the same.

In your Bible, read **Mark 6:7-12, 31-32.** Why did Jesus tell His disciples to find a solitary place? (v. 31)

_____

_____

_____

Jesus made people His top priority. He came to earth, He served, He suffered, and He died, *for people.* He was quite literally the embodiment of love, the exact representation of the Father. (See **John 14:9, Colossians 1:15, Hebrews 1:3**). He did nothing on His own, *but only what He saw the Father do.* He said nothing on His own, *but only what He heard the Father say.* (See **John 5:19, John 8:28-29, and John 12:49**) So, in order to fulfill the mission for which He came—in order to serve the very people He loved—He needed to be able to hear the Father. Therefore, He made it a priority to pull away from the people and create space for the Father to speak to Him. **One of the most loving acts we can perform for our people is to pull away from the noise of life so we can make room in our thoughts to hear God speak.**

"Inward solitude has outward manifestations. There is the freedom to be alone, not in order to be away from people, but in order to hear the divine Whisper better."
Richard Foster[22]

DIG DEEPER: In your Bible read the verses mentioned in the previous paragraph. Take some time to meditate on the truths that Jesus was the exact representation of the Father and that He only said what He heard the Father say. What jumps out at you? What questions do you have for God? Record any thoughts you have here:

_____

_____

_____

_____

Maybe you're not a fan of silence. Maybe the mere thought of sitting in complete silence for any length of time is unbearable to you—perhaps, even scary. My daughter is like this. She hates silence. She can't do her homework without music playing. I marvel at her ability to complete middle school algebra equations correctly with the *Hamilton* soundtrack playing on the computer. She reads with the TV on for background noise. If she's not listening to music, she's singing. If she's not singing, she's talking. She falls asleep every night to music. If I sneak into her room to turn the music off, she wakes up and turns it back on.

REFLECT AND ASSESS

If the idea of integrating periods of solitude into your life is uncomfortable for you, why is this? Check all that apply and/or write your own reason(s):

☐ **I hate being bored**

☐ **I get lonely**

☐ **I don't want to hear my own thoughts**

☐ **It drains my energy (I'm an extrovert)**

☐ **I have too much to do**

☐ **It's a waste of time**

☐ **I feel guilty**

☐ **I fear missing out on something better**

☐ **I'm afraid someone will need me and I won't be available**

☐ **Other:**

_____

_____

_____

If you find yourself avoiding solitude, you're probably straining to understand why it is necessary at all. So, consider the following ways that periods of solitude can help you hear the voice of God:

1. Solitude proves that God does not value us based on what we produce. This is a huge one for me. I love being productive, and most days I'm good at it. I'm naturally organized, I'm a self-starter, and I know how to get things done. Basically, I don't need anyone following behind me to hold me accountable. It's one of the things I like best about me.

But sometimes I think it's also *what God likes best about me.* Sometimes I believe the lie that God is most pleased with me when I'm useful. In fact, sometimes I believe that God is *only* pleased with me when I'm useful. It's a very deep internal struggle that's difficult for me to articulate, yet nags at me every time I attempt to rest.

In solitude, I force myself to set aside my to-do list, my calendar, my unanswered emails, and my phone. I cannot be productive or useful in any earthly sense. In fact, it's the opposite of productive. My only job is to sit quietly, and listen. Often in times of solitude, I need to remind myself that this is not a waste of time, but rather time well-spent. This releases my mind to accept what God actually values in me.

Does this resonate with you? Yes/No

If yes, explain:

_____

_____

2. Solitude creates spiritual hunger. We are a society of snackers. In the most literal sense of the word, we eat food all day long. Food is available everywhere we go. Need gas? Here's a bag of chips to go with that. Little league baseball game? Don't forget peanuts at the concession stand. Catching up with an old friend? Let's grab lunch. Business meeting? Donuts! Church? Stop by the coffee bar on the way to the sanctuary. Most of us have never experienced true physical hunger a day in our lives. We've been led to believe that any sense of hunger—even a hint of stomach-grumbling—is utterly unacceptable and must be suppressed immediately (or proactively) with food.

Hunger is a vital physiological response telling us that we need food. In fact, if one of my kids loses his or her appetite, I know something is wrong: either they are getting sick or they ate something that suppressed their appetite for the healthy meal I prepared. Healthy kids are hungry kids.

Solitude creates hunger in the spirit-realm. If we are constantly snacking on media, incessantly filling our ears and our brains with stimuli, we will never be hungry for the spiritual nourishment God is providing for us. We will just be overfed, undernourished Christians.

Does this resonate with you? Yes/No

If yes, explain:

_____

_____

3. Solitude combats hurry. Hurry is the earmark of our culture. It's sometimes associated with productivity, but it's sometimes just *rushing*. We are frustrated when the website takes longer than three seconds to load or if there's more than one customer ahead of us in the checkout. We are weaving in and out of traffic, flashing our brights behind every driver, not because we have a medical emergency, but because no one is moving fast enough. If someone doesn't respond to our text instantly, we text again. We simply cannot fathom cooking a meal at home, because *who has the time*?

Mark Buchanan in his book *The Rest of God* notes that the Swahili word for "white man" is *mazungu*—which literally means "one who spins around." That's how East Africans see Westerners: turning ourselves dizzy, a great whirl of motion without direction. As Buchanan so aptly states, "We're flurries going nowhere."[23]

Solitude repels all of this. It invites us to release the tension across our shoulders and the clench in our jaw. It shows us that the universe won't go into a holding pattern because we've stepped out for a moment to be with Jesus. Solitude reminds us that God isn't rushing, so maybe we shouldn't either.[24] Slowing down at any point in the day is helpful, but morning solitude in particular has the added benefit of setting an unhurried pace for the entire day.

Does this resonate with you? Yes/No

If yes, explain:

_____

_____

4. Solitude allows for deeper connection to God. By the time you read this, Jon and I will have been married for 27 years and will have known each other for 35. That's a long time, by any standard. We didn't stay married for this long accidentally—well, happily married, anyway. A neglected marriage is a dead marriage. Too many external factors fight against it—especially in our current climate, where marriage has been redefined and devalued, where it's "just a piece of paper" rather than a holy covenant before God. Add to that, selfishness and insecurity, pride and fear. And also, extended family and past relationships and unmet expectations. Not to mention the factors we've already named, like busyness and hurry, which can be caused or exacerbated by work and kids and finances.

What I'm saying is, to achieve any semblance of intimacy in marriage, a couple must proactively combat the external factors. And one way Jon and I achieve this is by taking care to carve out regular periods of time to connect and communicate beyond the daily activity of family life.

It's the difference between running errands with the kids strapped in the back seat, versus taking a trip alone as a couple. Or the difference between mornings in the kitchen—grabbing breakfast and backpacks and cell phones, while everyone is getting ready to rush out the door— versus a quiet dinner alone on date night. Or the difference between sitting around the chaotic and messy dinner table as a family, versus cuddling on the couch after the kids are in bed. Both are important, but they are two different levels of connection. Trust me, we screwed it up enough times over the last three decades to know that, if all we do is the busy-on-the-go communication, we will sacrifice intimacy and slowly drift away from each other.

"My soul waits in silence for God only; From Him is my salvation.
He only is my rock and my salvation, My stronghold;
I shall not be greatly shaken."
Psalm 62:1-2 NASB

The same factors that challenge intimacy and longevity in my marriage also fight against intimacy and longevity in my relationship with God. We can and should talk to God all day long. Because God is omnipresent, we can chat with Him on the go whenever we want. It's awesome. I do that all the time. But if that's all we do—talk to Him on the go—we sacrifice intimacy. And eventually, we will begin to drift away from God. There are simply too many factors fighting against it.

Does this resonate with you? Yes/No

If yes, explain:

_____

_____

If you have not yet developed the spiritual discipline of daily solitude, think through your daily routine. When might you carve out a period of time on a regular basis to pull away and be alone with God? It can be anywhere, anytime as long as it's quiet and a place you can visit daily.

Can you get up 15 minutes earlier? ☐

Can you stay up 15 minutes later? ☐

Do you have a morning or afternoon commute? ☐

Can you go for a walk or sit in your car during your lunch break? ☐

A P P L Y

Do your children take a nap? ☐

Can you close your bedroom door for 30 minutes while the kids do homework? ☐

Can you arrive to work a few minutes early and shut your office door? ☐

(P.S. If you don't think you have 30 minutes to spare, consider time you normally pick up your phone or stream your favorite TV series and start there. Remember, the average person spends over three hours a day on their phone!)

Make a commitment to God right now and tell Him where you will sit in solitude with Him tomorrow:

_____

_____

"I think for anyone who wants to live a spiritual life, solitude is essential."

Fr. Henri Nouwen

KEY #4: EMULATE A SPIRIT OF HUMILITY

From what I can tell, God talked to Moses more frequently, with more clarity, and in greater detail than He talked to anyone else recorded in scripture.

Consider:

- Moses received detailed instructions on how to approach Pharaoh and how to eventually lead the Jews out of Egyptian slavery and into the Promised Land.

- He heard from God regularly and clearly during the 40 years of wandering in the wilderness.

- He received the entire law directly from God and recorded it.

- He wrote the first five books of the Bible (Genesis, Exodus, Leviticus, Numbers, Deuteronomy—known as The Torah or The Pentateuch), Psalm 90, and possibly the book of Job, as the Holy Spirit inspired him.

To be sure, Moses knew how to listen to God. But what made him such a great listener?

In your Bible, read **Numbers 12** (the entire chapter) and answer the following questions:

1. What was the complaint Miriam and Aaron had against Moses? (v. 1)

_____

2. But what did they **actually say** against Moses? What was their underlying issue? (v. 2)

_____

3. Put a bookmark in **Numbers** 12 (we're coming back here) and turn to **Exodus 4:13** (you can read all of Exodus 3 and 4 for context). What was Moses' response when God originally called him to lead the Jews out of Egypt?

_____

_____

4. Now read **Numbers 11:24-30**. What was Moses' response when God took part of the power of the Spirit from him and gave it to the seventy elders? (v. 29)

_____

_____

5. Turn back to **Numbers 12:3** and write it out word-for-word:

_____

_____

By the way, Moses wrote the book of Numbers. So, I get a little tickled when I see the most humble man on earth telling everyone that he was, in fact, the most humble man on earth. That doesn't sound very humble, does it? This parenthetical phrase suggests that perhaps another author or editor of the book, inspired by the Holy Spirit, added a simple statement about Moses' character, probably to alert the reader to the absurdity of the accusations against him. Other commentators suggest that God inspired Moses to write this true statement about himself; and because it is true, it is not boastful. Whether Moses wrote it or not, notice how Moses makes no attempt to vindicate himself and how swiftly God comes to Moses' defense!

6. God stated that He spoke to Moses differently than He spoke to anyone else (vv. 6-8). How was it different?

_____

_____

_____

_____

7. What else did God say about Moses' character? (v. 7)

_____

Though Miriam and Aaron were paired together in this incident, the Hebrew verb translated "talk against" or "criticize" in verse one is in the feminine singular form, suggesting that Miriam was probably the instigator here, and explains why she received such a harsh punishment. But here are the important things to note:

- The sin of jealousy is very serious—especially jealousy as a result of God giving good things (in this case, the ability to hear God's voice) to others.

- God alone decides how, when, and to whom He will communicate.

- God will defend the innocent, the faithful, and the humble.

God is drawn to humility. He reveres those who possess it. He speaks more frequently and more clearly to those who emulate it. Whereas God is repulsed and repelled by pride, He draws close to those who choose to humble themselves before Him. In Isaiah 66:2, the Lord says, *"This is the one I esteem: he who is humble and contrite in spirit, and trembles at my word."*

I have an acquaintance whose auto-response to everything I say to him is, "I know." I can be talking about anything—cooking, theology, parenting, writing, car maintenance, thermonuclear engineering[25]— and he will respond with "I know." Have you ever tried to have a conversation with a know-it-all? It's maddening. They cut you off mid-sentence. They try to finish your thoughts. They often say, "Well, actually..." to correct you. Their words, their tone, their body language all communicate, "You cannot tell me anything I don't already know." I don't much enjoy talking to know-it-alls. I suppose this is the essence, at least in part, of why God opposes the proud but shows favor to the humble (**James 4:6**).

But there is something beautifully attractive about a humble person, not the least of which is the fact that they are teachable. As the leader of the women's ministry at my church, I serve women ages 18 to 80. I'll admit that I'm often intimidated when our older, wiser ladies show up to hear me teach or speak. They've been walking with the Lord longer than I've been alive. They have infinitely more life experience than I have had. What in the world can I possibly teach them? They should be teaching me. And yet, there they are, leaning in with open ears, eager to learn. I'm guessing this is why they are so wise to begin with.

REFLECT AND ASSESS

Think of a humble person in your life. What do you love most about her or him? How do you feel when you are around her or him?

_____

_____

_____

_____

_____

_____

In your Bible look up the following Scriptures about humility and answer the questions that follow:

Proverbs 11:2   **Proverbs 15:33**   **Proverbs 22:4**

1. How are wisdom and humility connected?

_____

_____

2. What are some other benefits of humility?

_____

_____

While we're discussing humility, let's revisit Daniel for a moment. Recall that we first met Daniel in Lesson Three when we talked about his deep love for the Lord. We learned how God often spoke to Daniel through visions and dreams and allowed Daniel to also interpret those visions and dreams (others' as well as his own).

Now, in Daniel chapter 10 we'll read about one of these times. Daniel received a vision about a great war. Seeking to understand its meaning, Daniel inquired of the Lord.

In your Bible, read **Daniel 10:1-14** about this encounter and answer the questions that follow.

1. How long did Daniel fast and pray before he heard from God? (vv. 2-3)

_____

_____

2. How did God choose to speak to Daniel to interpret the vision? (vv. 5-7)

_____

_____

3. What two things did Daniel do that caught God's attention? (v. 12)

_____

_____

4. We know Daniel fasted for three weeks, but how long did it take for God to hear Daniel? (v. 12)

_____

_____

5. Why didn't Daniel receive an answer to his prayer on the very first day? (v. 13)

_____

_____

This story is fascinating. I've gone back to it several times in my own walk with God when an answer to prayer failed to come as quickly as I hoped. It helps me remember that we are often dealing with things in the spirit-realm that we cannot discern without God's help. We will talk more about God's delay and silence later in the book, but today I want to note the following about Daniel's humility as demonstrated in this story:

* When Daniel wanted to hear God, he went on a fast.

* God saw the act of fasting as Daniel's way of "seeking understanding" and "humbling himself" before God.

* However, fasting does not always mean we are "humble." (See **Matt 6:1-18** for Jesus' teaching on this)

How to Emulate Humility

Jesus was the consummate example of humility. He taught on it extensively and modeled it flawlessly. So, in the simplest terms, when we emulate Jesus, we emulate humility.

In your Bible, read **Philippians 2:3-9**. How did Jesus humble Himself?

_____

_____

Read the following Scriptures and note briefly what Jesus taught regarding Himself and/or humility:

Matt 11:29 _____

Matt 18:2-4 _____

Matt 23:11-12 and Luke 9:48 _____

Luke 14:7-11 _____

Luke 18:9-17 _____

John 13:1-5 _____

Read the following verses. Though the word "humble" does not appear in any of them, they all describe one way Jesus consistently demonstrated humility. What is that one way?

John 5:19, 30, 41   **John 8:28, 42, 50**

John 6:38   **John 14:10, 24**

John 7:16, 28   _____

To be clear, humility *is not*...

- self-deprecation.

- self-hate.

- groveling, being a doormat, or allowing others to intimidate or control us.

- the absence of healthy boundaries around our time, energy, or resources.

- being timid or withdrawn.

Or as Rick Warren so aptly put it: "Humility is not thinking less of yourself, but thinking of yourself less."[26]

CS Lewis in his book *Mere Christianity* tells us how to recognize a humble person:

"Do not imagine that if you meet a really humble man he will be what most people call 'humble' nowadays: he will not be a sort of greasy, smarmy person, who is always telling you that, of course, he is nobody. Probably all you will think about him is that he seemed a cheerful, intelligent chap who took a real interest in what you said to him. If you do dislike him it will be because you feel a little envious of anyone who seems to enjoy life so easily. He will not be thinking about humility: he will not be thinking about himself at all.

If anyone would like to acquire humility, I can, I think, tell him the first step. The first step is to realise that one is proud. And a biggish step, too. At least, nothing whatever can be done before it. If you think you are not conceited, it means you are very conceited indeed."[27]

The Apostle Paul also taught extensively on humility. In your Bible, read the following verses. What does humility look like in everyday life according to Paul? (At first glance, some of these verses may not appear to be talking about humility!)

Romans 12:10, 16 _____

I Corinthians 13:4-5 _____

2 Corinthians 12:1-10 _____

Galatians 5:13, 22 _____

Ephesians 4:1-2 _____

Philippians 2:3-4 _____

Philippians 2:5-11 _____

Colossians 3:12-13 _____

"Oh, beware of the mistake so many make who would like to be humble but are afraid to be too humble. They have so many qualifications and limitations, so many reasonings and questionings, as to what true humility is to be and to do, that they never unreservedly yield themselves to it. Beware of this. Humble yourself to the point of death. It is in the death of self that humility is perfected."

Andrew Murray[28]

SUMMARY

- Moses was the most humble man on earth. God spoke to him like one speaks to a friend.

- Daniel demonstrated humility by going on an extended fast to seek understanding from God.

- Jesus is our perfect example of humility—He was God, yet took on flesh, became a servant, washed feet, and was obedient to death on the cross. He also continually pointed everyone back to the Father.

- Jesus taught extensively on humility, telling us to become like children and to refuse to seek honor on earth.

- Paul taught several practical ways to live out a life of humility including favoring others over ourselves, being patient, refusing to exalt ourselves, being willing to serve, maintaining unity, and freely forgiving.

Can you think of a challenging situation in your life right now where you can take a posture of humility? What does humility look like in that situation?

A
P
P
L
Y
_____

_____

_____

_____

_____

🔊 **Pause and Listen:** What do you hear God saying to you? If you don't "hear" anything, keep in mind that God most often speaks to us through the Bible, and the verses that "jump out" at us are oftentimes God directing our attention there. Write whatever you think God might be saying to you:

_____

_____

_____

_____

_____

_____

_____

_____

_____

_____

_____

_____

_____

FOR DISCUSSION

* What is your biggest challenge with incorporating periods of solitude into your day? If you don't find this to be a personal challenge, how might you encourage another woman who struggles in this area?

_____

_____

_____

_____

_____

_____

_____

_____

_____

_____

_____

_____

_____

_____

_____

_____

_____

_____

❀   What themes, practices, or concepts do you see repeated in the verses we studied on humility? What other virtues do you see closely associated with humility?

_____

_____

_____

_____

_____

_____

_____

_____

_____

_____

_____

_____

_____

_____

_____

_____

_____

_____

❋   What was your biggest takeaway from this lesson?

_____

_____

_____

_____

_____

_____

_____

_____

_____

_____

_____

_____

_____

_____

_____

_____

_____

_____

_____

Lesson Five

The 5 Keys to Becoming a Good Listener (cont.)

DEMONSTRATE A LIFE OF OBEDIENCE

"After removing Saul, he made David their king. God testified concerning him: 'I have found David son of Jesse, a man after my own heart; he will do everything I want him to do.'"

ACTS 13:22

I have a vivid memory from elementary school—maybe second or third grade. Our teacher handed out a worksheet to each student. As she walked around the room, placing the papers facedown on our desks, she gave us three simple instructions:

1. Wait until the entire class receives a paper before turning it over.

2. Be sure to read the instructions at the top of the paper *carefully* before you begin.

3. Bring your paper to the teacher's desk when you are finished.

Simple, right?

At her signal, we all turned over our papers. At the very top the instructions read, "READ ALL THE QUESTIONS BEFORE YOU BEGIN. DO NOT ANSWER ANY QUESTIONS UNTIL YOU'VE READ ALL THE WAY TO THE END."

I started reading through each question, as instructed. I don't remember how many questions there were, but I do remember the questions ran the length of the paper. I also remember thinking that the questions were complicated and time-consuming. I was nervous that I'd be working on this assignment for a long time.

I peeked around the room and saw my 8-year-old classmates feverishly scribbling answers to the questions. *What are they doing? How did they already read the questions? Cheaters.*

I continued reading all the questions as the instructions indicated, because in 3rd grade I was nothing if not a diehard rule-follower. Still am.

When I got to the end of the paper, I smiled. Without going back to answer a single question, I put down my pencil and confidently walked my paper to the front of the room. Before long, another student walked up. Then another. Eventually, about half of us were turning in our papers without having answered any questions.

Meanwhile, the other half of the class continued working, shifting restlessly in their seats. The questions were taking them so long to answer. I'm sure they were befuddled as to why half the class finished in a matter of minutes.

Those of us who finished giggled and exchanged glances. We obviously knew something the rest of the class did not. I was super proud of myself for following the directions. Still am.

The teacher waited, for what must have seemed to be an eternity, for the rest of the class to complete the assignment. One-by-one, we heard the audible groan of the remaining students as they completed the last question and then read the final statement at the bottom of the paper, the statement they would have read, if only they had followed the directions:

"Do not answer any of the questions! Put down your pencil and turn in your paper."

We are about to discuss the final key to becoming a good listener, but before we do, can you recall the first four?

The 5 Keys to Becoming a Good Listener

❀ Cultivate _____

❀ Saturate _____

❀ Integrate _____

❀ Emulate _____

❀ Demonstrate a Life of Obedience

KEY #5: DEMONSTRATE A LIFE OF OBEDIENCE

The final Key to Becoming a Good Listener is demonstrating a life of obedience. Our willingness to obey God and His specific instructions to us through His word are vital to hearing his voice. We must approach Him with the attitude of "I will obey whatever you tell me to do."

The converse of that is also true: Refusal to obey His commands or not following God's specific instructions to us—even if they seem unnecessary or senseless to us—will prevent us from hearing His voice.

Ezekiel 12:1-2 says, "The word of the Lord came to me: 'Son of man, you are living among a rebellious people. They have eyes to see but do not see and **ears to hear but do not hear, for they are a rebellious people**.'" (Emphasis mine.)

Obedience in the Old Testament

In the Old Testament, the best place to understand obedience and disobedience to God is in the book of Deuteronomy. For many of us, when we hear "open to the book of Deuteronomy," we expect it to be as exciting and applicable as the dictionary. Useful? Sure. True? Absolutely. Interesting? Hardly.

I used to think the same thing, until I actually studied it. Now it is one of my favorite books in all of Scripture. I hope it's the same for you when we are finished.

Allow me to offer you some context before we dive in.

The year is 1407 BC. The place is east of the Jordan River with the Promised Land in view. After 40 years of rebellion and frustration in the wilderness, the Children of Israel are finally ready to inherit the land of Canaan that God promised them. Wise and full of years, Moses stands before them to give a series of speeches. This is Moses' Farewell Discourse—his last words before he died. In a Farewell Discourse, people say the most important things. These are their dying words, after all.

Moses begins in chapter one of Deuteronomy by reviewing with them everything that happened in the books of Exodus, Leviticus, and Numbers. He reminds them what happened since God delivered them from slavery in Egypt, and how God gave them the law on Mt. Sinai and how they had been wandering in the wilderness because of their rebellion.

Then Moses proceeds to review the law with them, beginning with the 10 Commandments, and the Shema—Hear O Israel, the Lord our God, the Lord is one. Love the Lord your God with all your heart, with all your soul and with all your strength—a command which would later be identified by Jesus as the "the first and greatest commandment." (See **Matthew 22** and **Mark 12**.)

And then Moses reads the entire law to the Children of Israel—for 22 long chapters (this part can totally get overwhelming, I get it!).

Through all this—reviewing their history and reviewing the Law—Moses is deeply concerned for Israel's uncompromising loyalty to Yahweh, their God, so he urges them repeatedly in these speeches to love God, obey Him, and be faithful to Him.

And then after reviewing the Law, Moses lays out the consequences of obedience to God and disobedience to God. That's where we will pick up the story.

In your Bible, turn to **Deuteronomy 28**.

1. Read verses 1-14 describing God's blessings for obedience. These are incredible benefits! Which of these blessings stand out to you? Write them here:

_____

_____

_____

2. Read verses 15-68 describing God's curses for disobedience. That's a hard read, isn't it? It's difficult for me to understand how the Children of Israel could know the consequences described here and still choose to disobey God. What are some reasons you think people choose to disobey God's commands, even when the consequences for doing so are clearly disastrous?

_____

_____

_____

The remainder of the Old Testament contains hundreds of stories where people either obeyed or rebelled against God, and reaped the consequences of their actions as outlined in **Deuteronomy 28**.

Obedience in the New Testament

Thankfully, we are under a new covenant, and we are not required to obey the Jewish law. But Jesus still requires obedience to His word and His commands.

In your Bible, read **Luke 6:46-49** and answer the questions that follow.

1. Jesus said it's not enough to simply hear His words. We must also

_____ . (v. 47)

2. Complete the chart columns below comparing the two houses described in this passage.

HOUSE ONE	HOUSE TWO
Hears the words of Jesus Yes/No	Hears the words of Jesus Yes/No
Puts them into practice? Yes/No	Puts them into practice? Yes/No
Dug _____	Built on the _____
Laid the _____ on a _____	Built without a _____
The flood came? Yes/No	The flood came? Yes/No
The house was _____ shaken	The house _____
The house was _____ built	_____ was complete

3. What similarities do you see between **Deuteronomy 28** and **Luke 6**? What differences do you see?

_____

_____

_____

Now let's look at a passage in **John 15** that shows how obedience to His commands relates specifically to hearing His voice. But before we go there, let me give a little context:

This chapter sits right in the middle of a longer conversation Jesus had with His disciples, beginning in **John 13** in the upper room, and continuing through to the end of **John 17** on the way to the Garden of Gethsemane just before Judas betrays Him in **John 18**. It is just before the Passover Festival and Jesus knows that the hour has come for Him to leave this world and go to the Father. He is no longer teaching publicly and He has only the chosen twelve around him for their last meal together. There, He proceeds to wash the disciples' feet, and then He dismisses Judas who leaves to betray Him.

Beginning in **John 14**, He talks only to the remaining eleven. He knows in just a few short hours He will die, and He gathers his very closest friends for His final instructions to them.

Picture yourself, if you knew you would be dying in a few hours, gathering around your very closest people—maybe your husband, if you're married, and your children, if you're a mother—your best friends, your family. You are trying to squeeze in the most important things you want them to know before you die. This is what is happening here. He is literally telling them the most important things they must know before He leaves them—some of the most vital and most tender words in the entire Bible.

With that as a backdrop, read **John 14:23-25** below and answer the questions that follow:

23 Jesus replied, "Anyone who loves me will obey my teaching. My Father will love them, and we will come to them and make our home with them. 24 Anyone who does not love me will not obey my teaching. These words you hear are not my own; they belong to the Father who sent me. 25 "All this I have spoken while still with you. 26 But the Advocate, the Holy Spirit, whom the Father will send in my name, will teach you all things and will remind you of everything I have said to you.

---

1. Jesus says in verse 23, "Anyone who loves me will _____ _____ _____" and in verse 24, "Anyone who does not love me will _____ _____ _____ _____."

2. Immediately following the instruction to obey Jesus' teaching, what does Jesus say the Holy Spirit will do for us? (V. 26)

_____

Now look at **John 15:9-15** below. This is part of that same conversation, Jesus' final words to his closest friends:

9 "As the Father has loved me, so have I loved you. Now remain in my love. **10** If you keep my commands, you will remain in my love, just as I have kept my Father's commands and remain in his love. **11** I have told you this so that my joy may be in you and that your joy may be complete. **12** My command is this: Love each other as I have loved you. **13** Greater love has no one than this: to lay down one's life for one's friends. **14** You are my friends if you do what I command. **15** I no longer call you servants, because a servant does not know his master's business. Instead, I have called you friends, for everything that I learned from my Father I have made known to you."

---

1. How do we remain in Jesus' love? (v.10)

_____

2. In verse 14, Jesus says, "You are my friends if you _____ _____ ___ _____."

3. In verse 15, what special benefit do Jesus' friends receive?

_____

Now in your Bible, turn to a related scripture in **James 2:14-24**.

1. What name did God give Abraham? (v.23)

_____

2. Based on this entire passage, why did Abraham receive this special designation?

_____

3. Do you remember someone else who was called God's friend? (Hint: Look back on the lesson about humility.)

_____

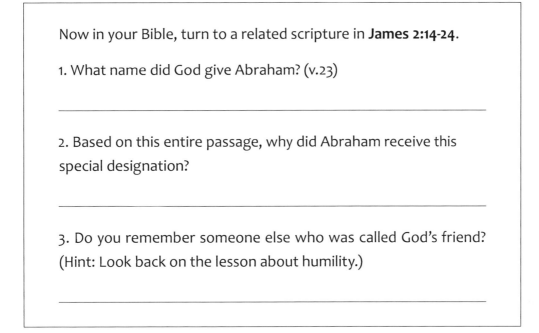 **DIG DEEPER:** Read John chapters 13-17 for the entire conversation Jesus had with his disciples before He was betrayed. Though this does not necessarily give us more insight on obedience, it is always beneficial to read passages of scripture within their larger context. Take note of anything that jumps out to you and any thoughts you have along the way.

Obedience Is Also the Key to Future Hearing

Since my kids were little, we've reserved an hour or two on Saturday mornings for family chores. I enjoy a clean, uncluttered house. It helps my brain breathe. I mean, I'm not a crazy person about it. I don't need my house to be spotless. We're not a magazine spread. But I prefer to strike a balance somewhere between "immaculate" and "health code violation."

Oftentimes, I will work on dusting, vacuuming, and mopping the main areas while the kids work on their rooms. This allows me to bask in the exactly five minutes where the entire house is mostly clean before someone gets hungry and dirties up the kitchen. In fact, as I write this lesson, it's Saturday morning, and I can hear water running and music blasting upstairs as Elliana and Elijah clean their bathrooms. It's a gorgeous sound.

It's not all rainbows and sunshine though, because my three kids approach chores differently.

My oldest daughter is completely capable, but hates doing chores. She resists and fights the entire process, but then, after putting in the blood/sweat/tears (I exaggerate only slightly), she ends up thrilled with the resulting tidy room. Before she moved into her own apartment, the condition of her bedroom was a perpetual point of contention between us. I don't know if she didn't see the dirt or didn't care about the dirt. But I saw it and I cared. I realize "cleanliness is next to godliness" is not in the Bible, but that doesn't mean it's untrue, is all I'm saying. We are both thankful that she now has her own place for this reason alone. She can keep her apartment as clean or as dirty as she wants it, and I don't have to see it. Win-win.

My youngest is both capable and willing to work. In fact, I'd go so far as to say she actually loves chores. She gets excited about various cleaning products and methods of organization. One time as a punishment for misbehavior, I told her she needed to wash the baseboards. She clapped and jumped up and down. She's my favorite child, obviously. I'm kidding. But, should I ever get to the point in my old age where I can no longer scrub the mildew out of my toilet, I choose Elliana.

My middle child is compliant, but not very capable—bless his heart. He always goes into Saturday chores with both good intentions and a great attitude, but without great skill. I hate to micromanage, but I often need to follow behind him asking, "Are you sure you cleaned that?" It's frustrating for both of us, trust me.

Here's another difference between my children and their approaches to chores: with my daughters, I can give them all their chores at once—put away your laundry, make your bed, wipe the bathroom sink, vacuum your bedroom, etc.—and I won't hear from them again until they are finished and free. But with my son, I can't do that. Since he has ADHD, a long verbal list of tasks sounds like a garbled mess of overwhelm to him. When he was small, he'd run off to go work on his chores with his sisters, but get distracted by Legos within the first five minutes. I'd have to give him one task at a time, literally. I'd tell him, "Go up stairs and make your bed. When you are finished, come back and tell me. Then I'll give you the next chore. Sometimes he'd come back for his next chore without having completed the chore I sent him to do because he forgot what it was. (ADHD and boys is no joke, man.) So, I'd have to send him back again, "Do the first chore and *then* I'll tell you what to do next."

> *"God doesn't speak to be heard; He speaks to be obeyed."*
> **Priscilla Shirer**[29]

If God has spoken something to you, He expects you to take it seriously and to obey it. And often, He will refrain from speaking to you any further until you obey what He's already said to you. Jesus taught this principle in **Luke 16**, saying that when we show faithfulness in the little things, God will entrust us with more. In that scripture, Jesus was speaking specifically about money. But the same principal can be applied here: when we show faithfulness with what He's entrusted to us—in this case, faithfulness to obey His word—He will tell us more. So, if you are having a difficult time hearing God, go back to the last thing you know (or think) He said to you and be sure that you have obeyed it.

🔊 **Pause and Listen:** What was the last instruction you believe God gave you? Was it a specific verse of Scripture? Was it a prompting to confess a sin? Forgive an offense? Confront an injustice? Speak the truth? Destroy an idol? Love an enemy? Take a thought into captivity and make it obedient to Christ? Write the last instruction here:

_____

_____

Your immediate obedience to that command will open up your ears to His voice again. Henry Blackaby says, "God's opinion is not just one of your options. God is not interested in debating with you about your best course of action. He already knows what that is. If you only respond to God on your terms and in your timing, then you are not prepared to hear from him."[30]

Pray Psalm 119:34 *"Give me understanding, and I will keep your law and obey it with all my heart."*

Write a prayer of commitment to God right now to obey what He's told you to do:

_____

_____

_____

Obedience and the Good Listeners of the Bible: Noah, David, and Elijah

Remember, God can and will speak to whomever He wants and however He chooses. But, as we already discussed in Lesson Three, those who walked closely with the Lord heard His voice most clearly and most often. Related to this (walking closely with God) is that those same people showed their love and devotion to God by having a heart to obey him. Let's continue this lesson on obedience by taking a look at what an obedient heart looked like for some of our Good Listeners.

Noah

Noah received intricately detailed instructions that would ultimately save his family from destruction and perpetuate civilization after the worldwide flood. In order to hear explicit instructions for such a massive project, Noah had to have been a great listener. We don't know a lot about Noah's daily walk with the Lord in his 950 years on this earth, but we do know enough to see why God entrusted Him with such important information.

In your Bible read **Genesis 6:5-22** then answer the following questions:

1. Fill in the blank for verse 8: "But Noah found _____ in the eyes of the Lord."

2. Genesis 6:9 tells us that Noah walked faithfully with God. Which of the 5 Keys to Becoming a Good Listener do you think this best describes? (Hint: it's not #5, so I eliminated this option for you.)
   1. Cultivate a Growing Relationship with God
   2. Saturate Your Mind with Scripture
   3. Integrate Periods of Solitude
   4. Emulate a Spirit of Humility
   5. ~~Demonstrate a Life of Obedience~~

3. Summarize the instructions given to Noah in Genesis 6:14-21.

Make an _____

The material: _____

The dimensions: _____

The roof: _____

The door: _____

The people to come inside the ark: _____

The other things to come into the ark with the people:

_____

4. Write **Genesis 6:22** word-for-word:

_____

_____

_____

5. Now read **Genesis 7:1-4** below and fill in the blanks for the detailed instructions (hint: all the blanks are numbers):

The Lord then said to Noah, "Go into the ark, you and your whole family, because I have found you righteous in this generation. 2 Take with you _____ pairs of every kind of clean animal, a male and its mate, and _____ pair of every kind of unclean animal, a male and its mate, 3 and also _____ pairs of every kind of bird, male and female, to keep their various kinds alive throughout the earth. 4 _____ days from now I will send rain on the earth for _____ days and _____ nights, and I will wipe from the face of the earth every living creature I have made."

6. Write **Genesis 7:5** word-for-word

_____

_____

_____

7. We know that everything happened just as God said it would— the animals, the rain, the flood, the destruction—all of it. After the water receded, God told Noah to come out of the ark and to bring his family and all the animals with him. What did Noah do in response? (Genesis 8:18-20):

_____

_____

_____

8. What is your biggest takeaway from Noah's example of obedience?

_____

_____

_____

David

Before we look again at David and his obedience, let's quickly look at Saul, the first king of Israel.

Read the following passages concerning Saul and answer the questions that follow:

I Samuel 13: 13-14   **I Samuel 15:10, 22-23**   **Acts 13:22**

Why was Saul rejected as king over Israel?

_____

Who was appointed in his place?

_____

Why was he appointed instead of Saul?

_____

Write out **Acts 13:22** word-for-word:

_____

_____

_____

_____

_____

_____

Did you catch that? God Himself called David "a man after my own heart" because David did everything God commanded him to do.

To be sure, David was not sinless, flawless, or blameless. He committed many sins—most notably adultery and murder. And yet, God said that David did everything that God asked of him. At first glance, this appears to be a contradiction. But perhaps this is more a statement describing David's heart and less a description describing David's actions. Personally, I find hope in this. God does not expect us to be perfectly sinless. Instead, He esteems the one who loves God's law and longs to obey it—the one who, when confronted with the reality of his sin, remains contrite before the Lord and turns back to God.

We've already looked closely at David's life in Lesson Three and we know that David walked with God from a young age. But the first recorded incident of David inquiring of the Lord and God answering David is in **I Samuel 23**. We're going to go there in a minute, but let me give you some context first:

David is running for his life from Saul. Saul, in his deadly and hateful pursuit of David, has just murdered 85 priests and the entire town of Nob (including men, women, children, infants, cattle, donkeys, and sheep). Saul committed this heinous act because Ahimelek, the priest in Nob, gave David bread and a weapon, thinking David was on a mission *for* Saul, not running *from* him.

Even while David is a fugitive, he is leading men, providing for the safety of his family, and defending cities against the Philistines, because David loves the Lord and is a man of integrity. And this is where we pick up this story.

Read the following passages below, taking note of the very specific questions David asks of God and God's very specific answers. **In bold you see all of God's specific directions to David.** Underline each of David's responses to God's commands.

1 Samuel 23:1-4

23 When David was told, "Look, the Philistines are fighting against Keilah and are looting the threshing floors," **2** he inquired of the Lord, saying, "Shall I go and attack these Philistines?"

The Lord answered him, **"Go, attack the Philistines and save Keilah."**

3 But David's men said to him, "Here in Judah we are afraid. How much more, then, if we go to Keilah against the Philistine forces!"

4 Once again David inquired of the Lord, and the Lord answered him, **"Go down to Keilah, for I am going to give the Philistines into your hand." 5** So David and his men went to Keilah, fought the Philistines and carried off their livestock. He inflicted heavy losses on the Philistines and saved the people of Keilah. **6** (Now Abiathar son of Ahimelek had brought the ephod down with him when he fled to David at Keilah.)

1 Samuel 30:7-8

7 *Then David said to Abiathar the priest, the son of Ahimelek, "Bring me the ephod." Abiathar brought it to him,* **8** *and David inquired of the Lord, "Shall I pursue this raiding party? Will I overtake them?"*

"Pursue them," *he answered.* **"You will certainly overtake them and succeed in the rescue."**

9 *David and the six hundred men with him came to the Besor Valley, where some stayed behind.* **10** *Two hundred of them were too exhausted to cross the valley, but David and the other four hundred continued the pursuit.*

2 Samuel 2:1-4

2 *In the course of time, David inquired of the Lord. "Shall I go up to one of the towns of Judah?" he asked.*

The Lord said, **"Go up."**

David asked, "Where shall I go?"

"To Hebron," *the Lord answered.*

2 *So David went up there with his two wives, Ahinoam of Jezreel and Abigail, the widow of Nabal of Carmel.* **3** *David also took the men who were with him, each with his family, and they settled in Hebron and its towns.* **4** *Then the men of Judah came to Hebron, and there they anointed David king over the tribe of Judah.*

2 Samuel 5:19-25

19 *so David inquired of the Lord, "Shall I go and attack the Philistines? Will you deliver them into my hands?"*

The Lord answered him, **"Go, for I will surely deliver the Philistines into your hands."**

20 *So David went to Baal Perazim, and there he defeated them. He said, "As waters break out, the Lord has broken out against my enemies before me." So that place was called Baal Perazim.* **21** *The Philistines abandoned their idols there, and David and his men carried them off.*

22 *Once more the Philistines came up and spread out in the Valley of Rephaim;* **23** *so David inquired of the Lord, and he answered,* **"Do not go straight up, but circle around behind them and attack them in front of the poplar trees. 24 As soon as you hear the sound of marching in the tops of the poplar trees, move quickly, because that will mean the Lord has gone out in front of you to strike the Philistine army."** **25** *So David did as the Lord commanded him, and he struck down the Philistines all the way from Gibeon to Gezer.*

What is your biggest takeaway from David's example of obedience?

_____

_____

_____

Elijah

The Prophet Elijah had some of the most notable encounters with hearing God's voice in all of Scripture. God used Elijah mightily and performed many miracles through him. We looked at some of these in Lesson Two when we were studying the different methods God uses to speak and the reasons why He speaks, but now we are going to focus specifically on Elijah's obedient responses.

Read **1 Kings 17-20** for context. Then go back to the following verses and answer the accompanying questions.

1 Kings 17:2-5

What did God say?

_____

What was Elijah's response?

_____

_____

1 Kings 17:8-10

What did God say?

_____

What was Elijah's response?

_____

_____

Write **1 Kings 17:24** word-for-word:

_____

_____

1 Kings 18:1-2

What did God say?

_____

What was Elijah's response?

_____

_____

Complete **1 Kings 18:46a:**

"The _____ _____ _____ _____

came on Elijah..."

1 Kings 19:5-6

What did God say (through the angel)?

_____

What was Elijah's response?

_____

_____

1 Kings 19:7-8

What did God say (through the angel a second time)?

_____

What was Elijah's response?

_____

_____

1 Kings 19:15-19

What did God say?

_____

What was Elijah's response?

_____

_____

What is your biggest takeaway from Elijah's example of obedience?

_____

_____

_____

_____

SUMMARY

- Our willingness to obey God is vital to hearing his voice.

- Disobedience to God's commands or instructions will prevent us from hearing His voice.

- The Old Testament contains hundreds of stories where people either obeyed or disobeyed God and reaped the consequences of their actions—good or bad.

- Jesus said that anyone who loves Him will keep His commandments. Love for God and obedience to Him are inseparable.

- If you are having a hard time hearing God, go back to the last thing you believe He said to you and make certain you have obeyed it.

- Noah, David, and Elijah were some of the best listeners in the Bible. They received highly detailed instructions from God and obeyed them meticulously and immediately.

As we conclude discussion on The 5 Five Keys to Becoming a Good Listener, it's imperative that I say this: these keys are interdependent on one another. They aren't neat and tidy categories. They intersect and overlap and intertwine. *Cultivating a Growing Relationship with God* cannot be separated from *Saturating Your Mind with Scripture*, because knowing Scripture is how we get to know God. *Cultivating a Growing Relationship* with God and *Saturating your Mind with Scripture* cannot be separated from *Integrating Periods of Solitude* because it is in the quiet places that we talk to God and consume His word. And truly, what's the point of knowing God's word and his will if we don't intend to obey it? And obviously, none of this works if we don't approach God with a posture of humility.

As a self-proclaimed List Girl, I'm tempted to view these as separate points to check off. Let's not do that. Instead, let's think of them as fibers in our favorite cozy sweater. You know the one, where you pull on one dangling string and the whole thing comes unraveled. Or maybe ingredients in a cake. They're all baked in there, you can't separate them, but if you skip one of the ingredients—even the seemingly pointless ones—your cake will be gross or fail to rise.

FOR DISCUSSION

✿ Though we are no longer under the law of the Old Testament, we still reap many consequences in this life (other than difficulty hearing God) when we walk in disobedience to God's commands. Consider Galatians 6:7-8 that says, "Do not be deceived: God cannot be mocked. A man reaps what he sows. Whoever sows to please their flesh, from the flesh will reap destruction; whoever sows to please the Spirit, from the Spirit will reap eternal life." Can you think of a time when you knowingly made a bad decision and reaped the consequences of it?

_____

_____

_____

_____

_____

_____

_____

_____

_____

_____

_____

_____

_____

_____

❀   Why do you think it appears some people do not suffer consequences even after they have clearly made choices contrary to Scripture?

_____

_____

_____

_____

_____

_____

_____

_____

_____

_____

_____

_____

_____

_____

_____

_____

_____

_____

_____

Jesus said in John 16:33 that we would have trouble in this world. Discuss how sometimes life's difficulties are not necessarily a result of our disobedience.

_____

_____

_____

_____

_____

_____

_____

_____

_____

_____

_____

_____

_____

_____

_____

_____

_____

_____

✿   What is your biggest takeaway from this lesson?

_____

_____

_____

_____

_____

_____

_____

_____

_____

_____

_____

_____

_____

_____

_____

_____

_____

_____

_____

_____

_____

Lesson Six

The Inner Voice

THE CONSCIENCE
PEACE

"I will praise the Lord, who counsels me; even at night my heart instructs me."

PSALM 16:7

January 4, 2008, my little family traveled to Guatemala to meet and bring home our fourth child. Elliana, our then 13-month-old daughter, lived in a Spanish-speaking foster home, in a Spanish-speaking city, in a Spanish-speaking country her entire short life. That is, until her lovely Spanish-speaking foster mother placed her in my arms in the lobby of the Spanish-speaking Westin Hotel.

You guys. I cannot speak Spanish *at all*. I'm a blonde Polish-German Yankee from the Midwest. I'm fluent in English and sarcasm. When we were in the adoption process, the only Spanish words I knew were *hola, adios,* and the contents of the Taco Bell menu. The latter of which proved to be rather helpful when we discovered her foster mother affectionately dubbed Elliana *Gordita*—which in Mexican cuisine, is a pastry made with masa and stuffed with cheese, meat, or other fillings— but literally means "Chubby Baby Girl."

To be clear, this would mean my new daughter would only understand me saying "hello," "goodbye," and "you're fat."

Oh, don't get me wrong. The nickname was both cute and accurate. And my Spanish-speaking friends assure me this kind of fat is a compliment—she was healthy and wellfed and carried some delicious rolls on those toddler thighs. Nonetheless, I decided against calling her "Chubby Baby Girl," for fear that I'd propel her straight into an eating disorder.

The first day or two in Guatemala were pitiful, as far as communication went. On day one, the cleaning lady and I stood at the threshold of my hotel room, staring at each other with apologetically furrowed brows, shaking our heads as if to say, "I have no idea what you are saying to me." (I had requested warm milk from room service. I'm still not sure what she wanted. Except she did not have my warm milk.)

I didn't know how to ask room service for anything. I didn't know how to say, "Which way to the grocery store?" or "What kind of meat is in this?" or "How do I get to the gym?" or "Pizza?" or "No ice, please." (This one proved to be unfortunate for the three of us who brought home stomach parasites from ingesting the contaminated water.)

The good news is that we spent seven days in Guatemala, surrounded by new friends, who were—thank you, Jesus— *bilingual.* I became a Spanish-speaking sponge, asking how to say words to my daughter that she could understand.

"How do you say, 'I'm sorry?'"

"Can you tell her that I love her?"

"How do I tell her she looks beautiful?"

Then, every night after we got Elliana to sleep, my husband and I would cuddle in the hotel bed with our older children (ages eight and six at the time) and giggle as we watched their favorite American TV shows dubbed in Spanish. Amazingly, as the week went on, I found myself understanding more and more of what they were saying in TV Land. As I listened to other people who were fluent in the language communicate with each other and with us, I started picking up certain words and phrases. **What had previously sounded like background noise or gibberish was beginning to sound like words and phrases.** I certainly wasn't anywhere near fluent by the end of the week, but I was surprised by how quickly I was picking it up...

And how quickly I lost it when we got back to the States! After only two months of no practice, I had forgotten almost everything I had learned. And Elliana had to rely solely on Dora the Explorer to retain her Spanish.

❋

2 Timothy 3:16 says, "All Scripture is given by inspiration of God, and is profitable for doctrine, for reproof, for correction, for instruction in righteousness."

The Bible is God's language—His native tongue. As we have already established, especially in Lesson Three, of all the truths concerning hearing God's voice, the most important one is that God will never lead you in a direction that is contrary to His written word. **God's voice and His word are inseparable**.

> Reread that last statement, and then write it again in your own handwriting:
>
> _____

In the Old Testament alone, the writers explicitly state over 3,800 times that they are conveying God's words. It's true that God alone has the power to open and close a person's ears to the sound of His voice. That means He can speak to whomever He wants. But as a general rule, you will have a very difficult time hearing God's voice if you don't familiarize yourself with His language. The more you read, hear, speak, write, memorize, study, seek to understand, teach, and sing God's word, the more you will discern His voice when He speaks to you.

In my personal experience, God uses His word to speak to me nearly every time He speaks, either directly through a passage I am reading, or by bringing a passage to my memory that I had previously read or heard. Jesus told us this is how it would happen.

In your Bible, read **John 14:25-26** and then write it here, word-for-word:

_____

_____

_____

Notice, Jesus said the Holy Spirit (Counselor or Advocate) would *teach* us and *remind* us of everything Jesus *already told us*. The Greek word translated "remind" in that verse literally means *to remember, to call to mind, to remind quietly, or to suggest to the memory.* It implies that *we already know something.* To the disciples, this meant the actual word Jesus spoke. To us, it means the Bible.

So, the Holy Spirit will speak to us quietly, calling His word to mind, suggesting His word *to our memory.* What happens then, if we don't have the Word of God in our hearts and minds to begin with? God will still speak to us. But if we aren't familiar with His language, we probably won't pay attention to what He is trying to say, because we may not even realize He is speaking! Just like my seven days in Guatemala, it wasn't that the people were not speaking at first. It was that their language meant absolutely nothing to me because I had no frame of reference for the meaning behind the syllables. It sounded like background noise. Over a week's time, as I started to learn phrases here and there, and started to recognize certain words I had heard repeatedly—even recognizing some French root words I had learned in high school—the language became real to me. I "heard" it, because I understood it and recognized something familiar.

REFLECT AND ASSESS **Have you ever studied a foreign language? What practices helped you become more fluent?**

_____

_____

_____

Using the principles of learning a foreign language that you just described, can you think of some practical ways to learn to hear the voice of God?

A
P
P
L
Y

_____

_____

_____

_____

_____

Before we go any further, let's quickly review. As we discussed in Lesson Two, God speaks to you for specific reasons. Remembering these reasons will be vital in learning to discern the inner voice. And alongside the written word of God, these will serve as a filter through which you can run what you hear.

Can you fill in the blanks from memory? (See Lesson Two if you need to peek.)

1. God wants you to know the truth about _____ .

2. God wants you to know the truth about _____ .

3. God wants you to know the truth about _____ and who they are.

4. God wants you to know what to do to further His _____ .

5.   God wants to tell you how and why to avoid _____
      (and whether or not you're in _____).

6.   God wants to tell you _____ .

7.   God wants your _____ to be transformed into His image.

8.   God wants you to _____ His name.

The Inner Voice in Scripture

Outside of God speaking to you directly through the written Word, the inner voice is the next most common way God will speak to you. We know this because it is also the most common way He spoke to people in Scripture. The Bible refers to it in many ways.

In your Bible, read the following passages and record the words used to describe the "inner voice." Use your favorite Bible translation. You may want to consult more than one. I've done the first one for you.

Luke 2:25-27

"Revealed by the Holy Spirit" and *"moved by the Spirit"* (NIV)

"The Spirit led him" (NLT)

"It was revealed unto him by the Holy Ghost" and *"he came by the spirit"* (KJV)

Acts 11:1-13 (Note, in verses 1-11, Peter is recounting the vision and it appears as though he heard an audible voice, but look specifically at verse 12 for the "inner voice.")

_____

_____

Acts 13:1-3

_____

_____

Acts 16:1-7 (specifically verses 6-7)

_____

_____

Romans 8:1-14 (specifically verse 14)

_____

_____

Galatians 5:16-18

_____

_____

If you are a Christian with the Spirit of God living in you, you have probably already "heard" the inner voice, but you may have referred to it as something else. _Have you used any of the following terms? Circle the ones you've used:_

❀ "I just knew it was right/wrong"

❀ Red light, green light, yellow light

❀ Red flag

❀ Gut feeling

❀ Intuition

❀ Conscience

❀ _Other:_ _____

The Conscience

Let's talk a minute about the conscience, because of all those terms up there, this one is actually found in Scripture.

First, a quick lesson about how we are made. We all have a physical body and a spiritual body. The physical body is our flesh and bones and organs and nerves and muscles. It's what we see when we look into the mirror. The spiritual body is our soul[31]—our mind, our will, and our emotions. The soul is what encompasses our personality, our ambitions, our likes, our dislikes, and our feelings about everything. The soul is essentially everything that makes us *us*, and it's also the part that lives for eternity after we die. It is, most importantly, the part uniquely designed by God for relationship with God—the part where the Spirit resides when we come to Christ.

The conscience is a part of the soul or the spiritual body. Its primary purpose is to help us determine what is morally good and morally bad, and ideally, it prompts us to choose the former rather than the latter. In the simplest terms, our conscience is our innate discernment. It is a loud voice in our head, trying to steer us in our choices. Everyone has a conscience—even non-believers—but not everyone is hearing the voice of God when they follow it.[32] So, how do we know when we are hearing God's voice or just our conscience? And, are those two voices ever the same?

Let's start by looking at some verses about the conscience to see some of the ways and under what circumstances "conscience" is described in Scripture.

Read the following passages in your Bible and then write the word(s) describing the conscience next to each one. I've done the first one for you. (To avoid confusion, you may want to consider consulting the NIV because the word is translated "conscience" in each of these verses.):

1 Samuel 24:5 David was conscience-stricken after cutting off the corner of Saul's robe

_____

2 Samuel 24:10

_____

Acts 23:1

_____

Acts 24:16

_____

1 Corinthians 8:7-12

_____

1 Timothy 3:8-9

_____

1 Timothy 4:1-2

_____

Titus 1:15

_____

Hebrews 9:13-14

_____

Hebrews 10:19-22

_____

Many things shape your conscience: parents, teachers, friends, society, even your previous choices and their resulting consequences help shape your conscience. If the influencers in your life have handled your conscience lovingly and wisely, you will generally grow up making right choices. This is why people who are not Christians can still be moral, kind, law-abiding citizens. Some of the nicest, most generous people I know are not Christians, and this is the reason.

If influencers have handled your conscience irresponsibly, abusively, inattentively, or recklessly, you will grow up making wrong choices. This is why people—even those raised "in the church"—can be, at the very least, broken and confused and, at the very worst, horrible human beings.

No conscience, no matter how "good" or "moral" can discern the voice of God all by itself. **All souls—and therefore, all consciences—apart from Christ are spiritually dead**. No matter how good your choices, if you are living apart from Christ, you are spiritually dead. This is why Jesus said, "Apart from Me you can do nothing." Obviously, you can do all kinds of things apart from Christ—good things, even—but those deeds will have no spiritual significance or eternal value, because your soul apart from Christ is spiritually dead. We can also *know* all kinds of things apart from Christ—good and smart things—**but we cannot discern the voice of God apart from the Spirit of God.**

In your Bible read **1 Corinthians 2** (the entire chapter).

1. To whom has the Spirit revealed "these things"? (v. 10)

_____

2. What are "these things" that have been revealed to us?

_____

3. If we are in the Church and are believers in Christ, what spirit have we received? (v. 12)

_____

4. What two things is Paul (the writer of 1 Corinthians) contrasting in verse 13?

_____

5. Write out verse 14, word-for-word:

_____

_____

6. Fill in the blank for verse 16:

for, "Who has known the mind of the Lord so as to instruct him?"

But we have _____ _____ _____.

When you surrender your life to Christ, He awakens your conscience to Him. At the point of conversion what was spiritually dead becomes alive. Then, when you begin the process of learning and obeying His commands, He takes your now-awakened conscience and remolds it and reshapes it. When you expose your newly awakened mind to Truth, your sense of right and wrong begins to align with what is *truly* right and wrong. Things you did not previously recognize as sinful or harmful now bother your conscience. And other things that previously left you feeling (wrongly) guilt-ridden, shameful, and condemned, are now powerless over you. God's word is reshaping your conscience to reflect Truth.

This is precisely why what (and whom!) we think about/meditate on/watch/listen to/read are vital to hearing God. These things and people shape our conscience and determine our ability to hear the inner voice through our conscience.

In your Bible, find **Romans 12:1-2**, and write it word-for-word here:

_____

_____

_____

_____

_____

_____

What happens when we are "transformed by the renewing of our minds?" (Look at the end of verse 2.)

_____

Think of it this way:

* Everyone is born with the "equipment" necessary to hear God's voice—that's our conscience.

* The equipment does not work properly until it's plugged into the power source—that's Jesus.

* With Jesus' power and our continual exposure and obedience to His word, the equipment can be fine-tuned and customized to more effectively discern God's voice. Through this fine-tuning, we can know God's good, pleasing, and perfect will.

Bottom line: we cannot follow our consciences apart from a relationship with Jesus. And we should be careful to hold everything our consciences say up to the authority of Scripture, especially when we are immature in the faith. The longer we walk with the Lord and the more mature we become, the more our conscience will align with God's Truth, and the more we can trust the inner voice.

Hebrews 5:13-14 makes this point when it says, *"Anyone who lives on milk, being still an infant, is not acquainted with the teaching about righteousness. But solid food is for the mature, who by constant use have trained themselves to distinguish good from evil."* The more we train our ear to hear the inner voice and then compare that voice to the Truth of God's word, the more easily we will learn to distinguish good from evil.

What or who are the primary influencers that have shaped your conscience, rightly or wrongly? This is a deep question, so take a few minutes to consider your answer. It may help to first think about one strong conviction you have and then name the influencer who shaped that in you. For example, I have a strong conviction to be loyal to my commitments, no matter what. This has caused me to feel guilt whenever I want to quit something, even if I have a valid reason. I can trace this back to my parents—particularly, my dad, who worked hard at the same factory job for over four decades to support his wife and seven children.

Now, your turn. Can you name a few of the primary influencers in your life? How did they shape your conscience?

_____

_____

_____

_____

_____

DIG DEEPER: Read the passages below about being "dead" or "alive" in Christ. Record any thoughts or insight you have as you read.

John 15:1-17

_____

Galatians 2:19-21

_____

Ephesians 2:1-10

_____

Colossians 2:13-15

_____

Peace

I've said it many times throughout this study, and I'll say it again: God's voice will never contradict God's word. That seems simple enough at face value. But you and I both know that most situations in life don't present themselves with a corresponding Scripture reference. Sure, you can find Scriptural *principles* to guide every decision. You can know, for example, that your motivation every day should be love for God and love for people (**Matthew 22:36-40**). That's a wonderful and worthy guide for all of us, always. But what does it mean to love God and love others when you're trying to decide...

where to send your kids to school?

where to work?

how much to spend on the family vacation?

whether or not to take on the new commitment?

which applicant to hire for your small business?

whether to have the elective surgery?

what house to buy?

where to set boundaries with your kids and technology?

how to tell your dad you're moving him to the assisted living facility?

Try as you might, you won't find a specific commandment about any of those things. **So, what do you do when the choice is not between good and evil, but between good and good? Or between neutral and neutral (and neutral and neutral and...)?**

Let's be honest here, isn't *this* the reason you picked up this Bible study to begin with? You aren't trying to decide between good and evil, are you? You aren't looking for a shortcut or an excuse to do whatever you want, right?

Right.

(I know this because you are now more than halfway through a Bible study on hearing God's voice. If you wanted an excuse to do whatever you want, you wouldn't be looking for it here.)

No, you are a decent human with a sincere desire to please God. You need help hearing God about your everyday, ordinary decisions—the big decisions and the little decisions affecting your family, your work, your health, and your time.

Yeah, me too.

That's why I'm so excited to tell you about the peace of God.

In your Bible read **Colossians 3** (the entire chapter) for context. Then write Colossians 3:15 word-for-word:

_____

_____

_____

Go back and circle the word "peace."

The Greek word translated "peace" is the word *eirēnē* (pronounced ā-rā'-nā). It can mean peace *with* God, the peace *of* God, or peace with *others*.

Notice how it is translated in the *Amplified Bible* and the *Amplified Bible, Classic Edition* below (emphasis mine):

15 Let **the peace of Christ [the inner calm of one who walks daily with Him]** *be the controlling factor in your hearts [deciding and settling questions that arise]. To this peace indeed you were called as members in one body [of believers]. And be thankful [to God always]. Colossians 3:15 (AMP)*

15 *And let* **the peace (soul harmony which comes) from Christ** *rule (act as umpire continually) in your hearts [deciding and settling with finality all questions that arise in your minds, in that peaceful state] to which as [members of Christ's] one body you were also called [to live]. And be thankful (appreciative), [giving praise to God always]. Colossians 3:15 (AMPCE)*

Here are some other ways *eirēnē* has been used in Scripture:

- A state of national tranquility

- Exemption from the rage and havoc of war

- Peace between individuals

- Security, safety, prosperity, felicity, (because peace and harmony make and keep things safe and prosperous)

- Of the Messiah's peace

- The way that leads to peace (salvation)

- Of Christianity, the tranquil state of a soul assured of its salvation through Christ, and so fearing nothing from God and content with its earthly lot, of whatsoever sort that is

- The blessed state of devout and upright men after death

Now go back to your handwritten verse of **Colossians 3:15** and underline the word "rule."

This Greek verb used here is the word *brabeuō* (pronounced brä-byü'-ō) and it literally means to "act as an umpire in an athletic contest" or to "arbitrate or decide." This is the only place this verb appears in Scripture. Notice how it is translated below (emphasis mine):

15 *Let the peace of Christ [the inner calm of one who walks daily with Him]* **be the controlling factor in your hearts [deciding and settling questions that arise].** *To this peace indeed you were called as members in one body [of believers]. And be thankful [to God always]. Colossians 3:15 (AMP)*

15 *And let the peace (soul harmony which comes) from Christ* **rule (act as umpire continually) in your hearts [deciding and settling with finality all questions that arise in your minds,** *in that peaceful state] to which as [members of Christ's] one body you were also called [to live]. And be thankful (appreciative), [giving praise to God always]. Colossians 3:15 (AMPCE)*

In addition to God bringing His word to our remembrance through our awakened conscience, God has also given us a built-in umpire to help us figure stuff out. It is the peace of God.

This is so exciting.

Think about the job of an umpire:

- ❀ He watches each play, each pitch, each swing, each pass, and each player crossing the plate. He chases them down the court, stands behind them at the plate, crouches and strains to see from his unique angle.

- ❀ He decides if the pitch is a foul or a strike.

- ❀ He determines if the runner is safe or out.

- ❀ He calls out a player or a ball if it strays out of bounds.

- ❀ He has studied the rules of the game—long before the game begins—and knows those rules inside and out.

- ❀ He realizes the rules are in place for many reasons, not the least of which is *for the safety of the players*—so they don't injure one another. The umpire keeps the players out of harmful situations.

* When a player breaks the rules, the umpire sits them on the bench.

* When a ruling must be made, it's not the coach, the players, or the fans who make it. It's the umpire.

Now, think about peace being your **umpire**. In every blank space below, write the word "peace":

* _____ watches carefully every thought, opportunity, action, suggestion, choice, or question.

* _____ chases us through life, stands behind us, where no one else is allowed to stand, crouches and strains to see what no one else can see.

* _____ decides if the opportunity is a foul or a strike (or a home run!).

* _____ determines if the thought is safe or out.

* _____ lets us know if our actions are out of bounds.

* _____ knows the rules of life (God's law), inside and out— long before life began, peace knew the rules.

* _____ realizes God's law is in place for many reasons, not the least of which is *for our good and for the good of others.*

* _____ keeps us out of harmful situations.

* When a ruling must be made, it's not the world, our flesh, our friends, or anything else that has the final say. It's _____!

Let's learn a little more about the peace of God. Look up each of the passages in the left column and then draw a line to what the passage teaches us about peace from the right column. (One of the passages points to two different answers.)

Psalm 85:8	Peace guards our hearts and minds
Psalm 119:165	Wisdom is peace-loving
Proverbs 14:30	God will lead us by His peace
Isaiah 9:6	When we sow peace we reap righteousness
Isaiah 26:3	The God of Peace is with us
Isaiah 55:12	Peace is a name of God
Romans 8:5-6	The Lord speaks/declares peace to His people
Galatians 5:22-23	The mind controlled by the Spirit is life and peace
Philippians 4:4-7	God's peace keeps us from stumbling or falling
Philippians 4:8-9	Peace transcends our understanding
James 3:13-17	A heart at peace gives life to the body
James 3:18	Peace is a by-product or fruit of the Spirit
	God gives peace to those who trust in Him

False Peace

Jesus said in John 14:27, *"Peace I leave with you; my peace I give you. I do not give to you* **as the world gives.** *Do not let your hearts be troubled and do not be afraid."* (Emphasis mine)

Jesus distinguished the peace He gives from the peace that the world gives. Over the years, I've had people tell me they feel "peace" about situations that I knew was not God's peace. I have had friends use "peace" as the reason they had an affair and left their marriage. In college, a guy I wasn't even dating and didn't even like told me he had a "peace" about us getting married. (Um, no.) They were feeling something, for sure. But it wasn't the peace of God. God's peace is sometimes hard to detect in us because it mimics other natural feelings.

It's especially difficult for me to detect God's peace *in you*. If you come to me for advice about a situation, and you tell me, "I have peace about this," I need more information before I can decide if it's God's peace or something else. I can listen for the tone in your voice and the words you choose to describe it. I can compare what you're telling me to what I know about God's truth. I can ask questions about how your choices will affect others. I can ask God to give me divine discernment about your situation. But at the end of the day, peace is something you must learn to discern in yourself.

Simply put, when you are on the right track, God gives peace liberally. When you are straying out of His will for you, He removes it. But we can't isolate peace and say, "I have peace, therefore God has spoken and I know this is the path for me." Peace works in tandem with every-thing else we've already studied. Remember the **5 Keys to Becoming a Good Listener**? Peace cannot be separated from all of that. Hearing God is not about checking boxes or following formulas. (*I read the Bible, check! I have peace, check!*) It's about a relationship with God. As you pursue God, you'll learn to better discern the peace of God—because true peace is a by-product of walking with God.

If you sense peace about a decision, ask yourself the following ques-tions to determine if it's the peace of God or peace from the world:

- Does this decision honor God and bring glory to Him?

- Is this decision rooted in love for other people?

- Does this decision promote unity and peace within the Body of Christ?

If the answer is yes to all three of those questions, then it is probably the peace of God.

Situations that Mimic God's Peace

For about three years, I was the Nursery and Preschool Director at my church in Florida. I had two small children at the time—babies, really—and worked on a volunteer basis. When I stepped into that role, I knew it was the perfect fit. I loved the work, the duties were in my wheelhouse, and I was honored to serve my newly-planted church in that way. But about two years into it, I started feeling like maybe I should step down.

Trying to work at the church with a toddler and a preschooler in tow was becoming more challenging. When I started, my son was a newborn in a car seat, and my daughter was a toddler who was content to sit quietly and look at board books while I worked. But as my son started crawling, it became apparent that he'd never be content to sit quietly while I worked—ever, for the rest of his life. No, he'd climb up every chair, table, and shelf. He'd open locked doors and cabinets and toilet seats. He'd eat Legos. He'd wander out of buildings and into parking lots. Keeping him alive was my new full-time job.

Sometimes I'd hire a babysitter to watch my kids so I could work at the church. But since I worked on a volunteer basis and was not drawing a paycheck to cover the cost of childcare, this put a strain on our finances. I mentioned earlier in this lesson that I have strong personal convictions about remaining loyal to my commitments (thank you, Dad), and I also have a strong work ethic (thank you again, Dad!). On top of that, I adored my pastor and his wife (still do) and didn't want to disappoint them or leave them without a director over their children's department. So, for months I powered through, even though I was spending the majority of my working hours trying to keep my son from destroying the church.

After almost a year of vacillating between continuing to serve as Nursery and Preschool Director and stepping down, I finally made the decision to give my notice. I remember sitting down with my pastors in my kitchen and explaining what I have just described to you. I probably cried a little. I knew this was not easy for them to understand, because most of the church staff—including them—had small children and were also working. I explained all my reasoning and how I had been wrestling with this for a full year. Then I said, "I really have peace about this."

My pastor looked at me from across the table and said, "Are you sure it's God's peace? Or are you just relieved because you've finally made a decision?"

Great question! And one that caused me to pause for a moment. I couldn't deny that it felt wonderful to finally have the dilemma resolved after struggling with it for so long. There's nothing wrong with that feeling. But *that feeling* was not the peace of God.

The peace of this world can mimic the peace of God. So as you seek to discern God's peace in your circumstance, consider whether what you are sensing is actually one or more of the following:

1. **Relief that a decision has been made.** I personally hate living in a state of indecision. This causes problems for me in my ability to discern peace. Sometimes if I wrestle with decisions for long periods of time, like the one I described to you, the simple act of reaching a decision can feel a lot like God's peace.

2. **Release from discomfort or responsibility.** When we leave an extremely uncomfortable or stressful situation, especially one that has been uncomfortable and stressful for a long time, we will feel "peace" when we escape it. To be fair, your life may be legitimately more *peaceful* when you walk away from a difficult circumstance. If you come home every night to screaming and fighting with your spouse, it will be more peaceful to move out. No question. But we cannot confuse "release" with God's peace. This can be especially dangerous when we are considering a job change, a relocation, or a divorce. For the record, God often *leads* us to endure painful trials and difficult circumstances. Rarely is the path of least resistance the path to God's will.[33]

In your Bible, find the following Scriptures and answer the questions that follow:

Exodus 13:17-18

1. Who did God lead?

_____

2. Where did God lead them?

_____

3. Why did God lead them that way?

_____

Matthew 4:1

1. Who did the Spirit lead?

_____

2. Where did the Spirit lead Him?

_____

3. Why did the Spirit lead Him there?

_____

---

3. **A met need: food, shelter, clothing, love, attention, affection.** Just because someone or something is meeting our needs, it does not necessarily mean it is God leading us there. If your husband is emotionally distant and another man is paying all kinds of attention to you, laughing at your jokes, asking about your dreams, and calling you beautiful, that may feel like peace, but I *guaran-darn-tee* you, it's not the peace of God. In fact, many times God leads us to a desolate place—a *needy* place—so that we will turn to Him and allow Him to be our sole Provider. He will use suffering to produce something more valuable in us.

In your Bible, find the following Scriptures. What does suffering produce in us, according to these passages?

Romans 5:1-5

_____

James 1:2-4

_____

1 Peter 1:6-7

_____

---

4. **A met desire: lust, wealth, power, fame.** Sometimes the lure of our flesh and the satisfaction of those desires feel so "right." When a new opportunity promises money or influence, we may confuse that with God's peace. Our flesh is one of the loudest, most persistent voices within us. It incessantly screams for attention. When we finally give in to what the flesh wants, it feels great—but, again, that is definitely not God's peace. It's very difficult to tell one from the other, which is why we devote Lesson Seven to "the voice of the flesh."

In case you're wondering what I did about the Nursery and Preschool Director job…

I followed through and gave my notice that day. I didn't know it at the time, but God was raising up another godly woman to replace me. And within a few months, God moved my family from Florida to Kentucky. This was one of the many circumstances God had lined up to position us for that relocation. So, while it *was* a good feeling to have made a decision, and it most certainly *was* release from a stressful situation, it was also the peace of God to lead us into His will.

A Word About Depression and Anxiety

One weekday morning while the kids were in school and Jon was at work, I was in my basement working out in front of the television to an exercise DVD, music blaring, when suddenly, our house alarm went off. We live on the back of a five-acre lot on the edge of the country, and I work from home. My worst fear is to be the victim of a home invasion when I'm here alone during the day.

So, I grabbed my phone and a giant knife (!) from a nearby drawer, locked myself in the bathroom closet, and waited for the alarm company to call. When the phone rang, I answered and heard Alarm Lady on the line.

Alarm Lady (AL): "This is the alarm company, are you okay?"

Me: "I don't know. I'm in the closet. The alarm is going off and I'm afraid to go upstairs."

AL: "Well, you need to go check, because we are showing multiple fire alarms going off."

Multiple fire alarms? Holy cow. But no home invasion. Thank God. I can deal with multiple fires, but I can't handle the thought of being murdered by an intruder.

I stood up and opened the bathroom door. With heart pounding and legs shaking, I could barely think…or walk.

Wobbly Me: "Please stay on the phone with me until I find the fire."

AL: "Of course."

I walked the stairway to the first floor. No fire. No smoke.

Master bedroom, closet, kitchen, living room.

Nothing.

The alarm piercing now, I approached the keypad to turn it off, but was so frazzled, I couldn't remember the code. I apologized to poor AL for what I'm sure was a terribly uncomfortable sound perforating her eardrum. Then I went up the second flight of stairs with my noodle legs and pounding heart to the kids' bedrooms to find the fire.

No fire. No smoke.

I went outside and walked the perimeter of the house.

No fire. No smoke.

AL waited until I checked the whole house inside and out. And then waited again as I finally remembered the code and turned off the alarm. Everything was fine. I hung up the phone and took a deep breath, trying to calm my body, *when suddenly…*

The alarm went off again!

AL called again.

Multiple fire alarms again.

My heart and my legs failed again.

I checked everything again.

No fire. No smoke.

Again.

This device, designed and installed to alert me of a life-threatening situation, was malfunctioning. We had a faulty sensor that needed attention. On her end, I had not one, but multiple fires in my home. On my end, it was a completely normal weekday morning.

❈

For those of us who struggle with clinical depression and anxiety, peace is complicated. There are times I am certain I am in the center of God's will for me, but my body is reacting as if I'm in major crisis or danger. I may be walking in love and obedience to God, but my body says, "Everything is terrible and wrong!" It's like having a faulty God-sensor. When I am suffering from severe depression or anxiety, I cannot hear God speak to me with peace. My traffic signal is stuck on flashing red. My inner alarm is malfunctioning.

This is when I can't rely on "peace" at all, because there is no peace. I know God is sending it, but I can't receive it.

In times like this, I must remain firmly planted in the Word of God, I must stay tethered to everything I know to be true, and I must remain very close to godly people who will speak Truth to me until my body catches up and my "sensors" start working properly again. I also need to implement radical self care.[34] For me, this involves being very kind to myself, eating the best foods, taking long walks, exercising daily, taking naps, going to bed early, avoiding stressful situations, and if necessary, seeking professional counseling. None of those things will bring God's peace. But they help my body and mind become healthy in a physical sense so I can properly discern peace in a spiritual sense.

SUMMARY

* God's voice sounds exactly like His word and will never contradict His word.

* Jesus promised to bring back to remembrance what He told us.

* Everyone has a conscience shaped by our environment, influencers, and experiences.

* Apart from Christ, our conscience is dead.

* At the point of conversion, our dead conscience becomes alive, allowing God to shape our conscience to align with His word.

* Most choices are not between good and evil, but between good and good.

* Most situations in life do not come to us with a corresponding Scripture reference.

* The peace of God acts as an umpire when we don't know what to do.

* The world mimics peace, so we must always ask these questions to discern if it's God's peace or false peace:

  * Does this decision honor God and bring glory to Him?

  * Is this decision rooted in love for other people?

  * Does this decision promote unity and peace within the Body of Christ?

* Peace is sometimes difficult to discern and is often misinterpreted. Therefore, it's best to confirm a "feeling of peace" with other ways God is speaking.

* Depression and anxiety can mute God's peace.

🔊 **Pause and Listen:**

What is a question or decision you are praying about right now?

_____

_____

_____

What are the potential answers or options you are considering?

_____

_____

Do your answers or options honor God and give glory to him?

_____

_____

_____

Are they rooted in love for other people?

_____

_____

_____

Do they promote unity in the Body of Christ?

_____

_____

_____

Can you eliminate any options after working through this lesson?

_____

_____

Do you feel the peace of God about any of these options?

_____

Ask God to speak to your heart right now. What do you hear God saying? (Write whatever you think and then ask Him to confirm it or clarify it.)

_____

_____

_____

_____

_____

_____

_____

_____

_____

_____

_____

_____

_____

_____

_____

_____

_____

FOR DISCUSSION

* Can you think of a time when you thought you had peace about something and it turned out it was not peace at all?

_____

_____

_____

_____

_____

_____

_____

_____

_____

_____

_____

_____

_____

_____

_____

_____

❀ Do you think you can have true peace and be afraid or scared at the same time? Can you think of a situation that was clearly God's will for you, but was also scary?

_____

_____

_____

_____

_____

_____

_____

_____

_____

_____

_____

_____

_____

_____

_____

_____

_____

What are some things you can do this week that will help you incline your ear to hear or sense God's peace?

_____

_____

_____

_____

_____

_____

_____

_____

_____

_____

_____

_____

_____

_____

_____

_____

_____

_____

_____

What was your biggest takeaway from this lesson?

_____

_____

_____

_____

_____

_____

_____

_____

_____

_____

_____

_____

_____

_____

_____

_____

_____

_____

_____

_____

_____

Lesson Seven

The Other Voices

THE FLESH AND EVIL SPIRITS

"Jesus said to him, "Away from me, Satan! For it is written: 'Worship the Lord your God, and serve him only.'"

MATTHEW 4:10

Dear Sandy,

I'm traveling in Germany and got robbed. I lose my wallet, my passport, and all luggage. I'm stranded in airport. Can you wire me money imediately?

God bless you.

Amy

Huh. This was odd. Why would Amy—5th grade room mom and wife of Elijah's intramural basketball coach—be emailing me asking for money? To be fair, her emails did usually include a money request—but it was more likely $20 for the teacher's birthday gift. Or cupcakes and water bottles for the class party. And how was Amy in Germany? Didn't I just pass her in carpool yesterday? And if she really was stranded in Germany, why didn't she contact her mom? Or her sister? Or the police? Also, do people still "wire" money, and if so, how does one accomplish this? And most importantly, when did Amy's grammar and spelling become so dreadful?

This did not sound like Amy.

I'm no Sherlock, but I concluded within 30 seconds that someone had hacked Amy's email account. At that point, it didn't matter who the hacker was—I had no intention to reply to this request or uncover his identity. The important information was as follows:

A. *This was not Amy.*

And

B. *I should ignore this email.*

According to various sources on the Internet, we have upwards of 70,000 thoughts per day. This translates to about 48 thoughts per minute. That's an overwhelming thought (ha!). But our brains are incredible in that they filter and sort these thoughts in such a way that we don't notice or retain the majority of them. They flow in and out of our minds without us even realizing. As we established in Lesson 5, some of those thoughts will be the Holy Spirit—God Himself—speaking directly to our conscience to poke and prod us along. Some of those thoughts will be God leading, comforting, encouraging, or warning by reminding us of what He's already spoken to us through His written word. And other thoughts will be God telling us something very specific to accomplish His purpose for His kingdom.

But what about the other tens of thousands of thoughts that come into our minds each day? Where do they come from, and what do we do with them? And is there a way for us to know for certain which thoughts are from God and which ones are not?

The very best way to recognize what **is not** God is to first learn what **is** God.

Remember, we can know exactly what God sounds like because we literally have His word, the Bible. By saturating our mind in Scripture (Key #2 for Becoming a Good Listener), we will eventually learn what God sounds like, and it will not matter what other voices are talking to us or what they are saying. We'll just know, *"That's not God."*

❁

To the untrained eye, counterfeit money looks exactly like the original. So, as part of routine training, bank employees must learn to identify which bills are counterfeit and which are authentic. But with the schemes and techniques of counterfeiters constantly changing and technology ever advancing, it's impossible for anyone to stay abreast of every single flawed marking. So, how do tellers learn to weed out the phony bills?

By studying the authentic ones.

Certain holographs, security threads, watermarks, and color-shifting ink only appear in authentic bills. And most of these markings can only been seen when they are held up to light or examined with a magnifying glass. Also, authentic bills feel different to the touch from counterfeit bills. So, tellers are trained to compare the look, feel, and texture of the paper in question with other bills they know to be authentic.

Counterfeit bills, if they're any good at all, will be similar to the authentic in many ways. But the U.S. Treasury instructs tellers *to look for differences in the bills*, not similarities. So, if a bill differs *in just one way from an authentic bill*, it's probably fake.[35]

Similarly, the most effective way to approach and identify the other voices in your head is to thoroughly train yourself to recognize the distinct qualities and feel of God's voice. When you hear a voice in your head, hold it up to the Light. Compare it to what you know to be true about God's motives and goals when He speaks. Examine it closely. How does this voice **feel** compared to God's word? If it differs **in just one way**, it's probably another voice.

This is precisely why we are spending seven lessons learning what God *does* sound like, and only one week talking about what He *doesn't*. Once you recognize God's voice, you won't need to identify all the other voices to know how to respond. In fact, in most cases, you won't need to respond to the other voice at all. The important information will be as follows:

A. *This is not God.*

And

B. *I should ignore this thought.*

REFLECT AND ASSESS

What are some of the authentic qualities of God's voice that you have learned so far? Can you recall His communication goals?

_____

_____

_____

_____

_____

_____

With that as a firm foundation, let's look at the two primary voices every human will hear besides the voice of God. Like God's voice, Scripture teaches us the distinct qualities of each voice and exactly how to respond to them.

The Flesh/Sinful Nature

The term "flesh," is not a word we see much these days. It was prevalent in older English translations of the Bible, but has largely been replaced by other terms in most modern English translations. Undoubtedly this shift is due to the wide variety of nuances the word "flesh" can have in the Biblical context that are better rendered by using other words.[36]

The original word translated "flesh" in the older translations of the Bible comes from the Hebrew word *basar* in the Old Testament or the Greek word *sarx* in the New Testament. Here are some of the many ways *basar* and *sarx* are used in Scripture—which may or may not appear as "flesh" in your translation (I've listed references if you want to look them up):

- The whole body: **Leviticus 14:9** and **Psalm 119:120**

- Human relationship (family): **Genesis 29:14**

- The body of an animal: **Genesis 41:1-3**

- Meat or food: **Exodus 21:28** and **Isaiah 22:13**

- Distinguishing physical existence (body) from spiritual existence (soul): **Isaiah 10:18** and **Psalm 63:1**

- General designation for all living things: **Genesis 6:17**

- All humanity: **Joel 2:28-32**

Other than being mortal and weak, none of these kinds of "flesh" are necessarily bad, wrong, or sinful. They are simply part of the normal, human experience. After all, Jesus had a fleshly body, had human fleshly relationships, was part of all fleshly humanity, and yet He was not bad, wrong, or sinful.

In the New Testament the term "flesh" takes on specialized theological meaning. Here we see "flesh" used to describe *the fallen sinful nature that controls human behavior and is counter to God's purpose.*[37]

Every one of us has a loud voice inside us that originates with this sinful nature. The bad news is we will all struggle with this voice until the day we die—when our physical body separates from our spiritual body forever. The good news is we can learn to recognize the distinct qualities of this voice so that we can silence it.

What does the voice of the flesh sound like?

In your Bible, find the passages below that describe the "voice of the flesh or the sinful nature." Then, write a brief description beside each one. You can choose from the phrases in the Word Bank below and add any of your own words. Many of the passages have more than one description that fits.

Word Bank

always wants something   *hates authority*

doesn't know what's best for it   *lacks self control*

never happy   *full of pride*

cannot be trusted   *selfish*

never satisfied

a slippery slope   *always seeks to justify its actions*

stubborn and unteachable   *always contrary to the Spirit*

deceptive   *tempts you to take the more*

dogmatic and legalistic   *comfortable way*

1. Jeremiah 17:9

_____

_____

_____

2. Matthew 26:41

_____

_____

_____

3. Romans 7:18

_____

_____

_____

4. Romans 8:7

_____

_____

_____

5. Galatians 5:16-21

_____

_____

_____

6. Philippians 3:3

_____

_____

_____

7. James 1:14-15

_____

_____

_____

8. 2 Peter 2:10

_____

_____

_____

9. 1 John 2:16

_____

_____

_____

Through those verses, we are able to begin to understand the roots, underlying motivations, or "tones" of the sinful nature. Those roots are not the thoughts themselves (i.e. You probably won't have the thought, "I am dogmatic and legalistic!"), but each root will *manifest into thoughts*. When my flesh or sinful nature is speaking to me, it says things like this:

What about me?

When am I going to get some time to myself?

Why am I always the last one to have my needs met?

Why are my plans always the ones that have to be changed?

I have every right to be angry right now.

I'll do it later.

Whatever.

Leave me alone.

I deserve this.

I'm so over this.

I'm done.

Whenever I "hear" any of those thoughts enter my mind, I pause. Not because I'm super-spiritual, but because I've learned that God doesn't say things like this to me. I've learned by trial and error that if I obey this voice—if I act on any of those thoughts and take them further—it does not lead to peace, love, or life. To the contrary, when I cater to this voice and its whining, it's a slippery slope that leads to sin—and sin eventually leads to death. In me, what starts as a simple thought from my flesh manifests as sinful behavior in one or more of these ways:

- Sleeping longer and more often than I should.

- Laziness.

- Procrastination on tasks God has told me to do.

- Gossip.

- Anger at people for inconveniencing me.

- Keeping a detailed record of how my husband has disappointed me.

- Yelling at my kids.

- Distancing myself emotionally or physically from my husband.

- Overanalyzing and overcomplicating situations.

- Being critical or judgmental of others.

- Justifying why I cannot fast even one meal.

- Relying on my own ability or talent rather than on God's power.

- Taking control over a situation instead of relying on or waiting for God.

- Shooting off a lengthy (albeit logical and well-written) email, text, or social media post justifying my position.

Maybe you're looking at that list and thinking, "This doesn't sound like my thoughts at all!" And you'd be correct. The voice of the flesh in *your* head will sound like *you*—only an ornery and contentious version of you.

(Or maybe you're thinking, "That sounds exactly like me!" In that case, nice to meet you—we are probably sisters separated at birth.)

Learning to recognize this voice takes time, because you've been thinking your fleshly thoughts your entire life. The root will always be the same—your sinful nature (the descriptions from the passages we looked at earlier). But the specifics will be unique to your personality, your tendencies, your fears, and your desires. Maybe your inner voice sounds more like fear and panic. Or depression and anxiety. Or pride and arrogance. Or loneliness and self-hate. Or jealousy and comparison. Or blame and judgment.

Remember, though, the best and most effective way to identify the voice of the flesh *is by knowing inside and out the voice of God*—the voice of love, peace, humility, contentment, gentleness, faith, and life. Your flesh will never sound like the voice of God.

🔊 **Pause and Listen:** Can you identify any words or phrases you hear in your mind—now or on a regular basis—that may be the voice of your flesh or sinful nature? Do you regularly have thoughts of fear? Thoughts of selfishness? Thoughts of pride? Thoughts of deception? Thoughts of legalism? Look over the descriptions of the flesh that you recorded earlier to prompt you. Pray and ask God to help you identify the specific thoughts. Then begin completing the chart below by following the steps.

Step One: Write the initial thoughts you have now or on a regular basis in the first column.

Step Two: Now next to each thought, can you describe what happens when you obey this voice? Does it lead to a sinful behavior? (This is a giant red flag that it is not the voice of God!) Write the behavior next to the thought in the second column. If you need more room, find a blank page at the end of this lesson or transfer this to a journal.

At the end of this lesson, we are going to respond to every one according to God's word in the third column.

Initial Thought	Sinful Action	My Response
Regularly thoughts of fear	worry, figure things out introspection	weary, confused depressed

How to Respond to the Voice of the Flesh

There is a wrong way and the right way to respond to this voice, according to Scripture. First, the wrong way:

1. Don't confuse the voice of your sinful nature with the legitimate needs of your physical body.

While we are on this earth, we all must care for our physical bodies. There is absolutely nothing sinful about taking good care of yourself.

In your Bible, find **Ephesians 5:25-33** for context, then write **verse 29** here, word-for-word:

_____

_____

_____

God does not expect us to deny ourselves of those things that bring physical health. In fact, He assumes that we will naturally take good care of ourselves, evidenced by the fact that He instructs husbands to love their wives the way they care for themselves. More importantly, God says that Christ loves the church in the same way we care for our bodies.

REFLECT AND ASSESS

How do you currently feel about "self-care"? Do you feel like it is self-indulgent? Unbiblical? Worldly? Frivolous? Or Necessary? Loving? Godly? Do you think "self-care" and taking care of yourself are the same things? Or do you draw a distinction between those terms? Explain your answer.

_____

_____

_____

_____

In your Bible, read **Matthew 6:25-34** and answer the questions below:

1. What human needs does Jesus describe in this passage?

_____

_____

2. What does Jesus instruct us to do with these needs? Circle the correct answer.

A. Ignore them.   C. Deny them.

B. Rebuke them.   D. Don't worry about them.

3. Explain in your own words how Jesus teaches us we can have our physical needs met.

_____

_____

_____

It is our duty as followers of Christ to take good care of ourselves. It is assumed in Scripture that we will eat healthy food, get proper rest, and acquire adequate shelter and clothing. Especially since we now know that most chronic and deadly diseases are preventable with healthy lifestyle choices. We become increasingly ineffective when we try to serve God and others from a place of exhaustion and self-imposed sickness. This is not how Christ treats His own Body. (We are His body, by the way.)

2. Don't try to handle the voice of the flesh by "rebuking" it.

This is sometimes a knee-jerk reaction to any voice that doesn't sound like God—just rebuke it in the name of Jesus. But when you try to silence your flesh by rebuking it, your flesh yawns and rolls its eyes at you. It doesn't work. (We're going to talk about the appropriate time to rebuke the voice on our head later in this lesson.)

3. Don't give in to the voice, whatever you do.

It will feel right and good at first to act on the voice of the flesh. In fact, it may even feel like God! But these good feelings will quickly dissipate and the original urge will eventually become unmanageable. It's like scratching a mosquito bite—feels great at first, but then it only itches more—or it bleeds and oozes and becomes infected. When we agree with the voice of the flesh and give in to it, the voice comes back stronger and louder. Think about every time you let your temper rage or you spilled all the juicy details about your friend or you flirted with the wrong guy—did it ever truly satisfy the initial desire? Or did it grow wildly out of control? You can be certain that giving in to the voice of the flesh always leads to stronger urges, greater temptations, and giant-er (it's a word) messes.

This is why **Romans 13:13-14** says

*"**13** Let us behave decently, as in the daytime, not in carousing and drunkenness, not in sexual immorality and debauchery, not in dissension and jealousy. **14** Rather, clothe yourselves with the Lord Jesus Christ, **and do not think about how to gratify the desires of the flesh.**" (Emphasis mine)*

Read **Romans 8:1-14** below and answer the questions that follow:

*Therefore, there is now no condemnation for those who are in Christ Jesus, **2** because through Christ Jesus the law of the Spirit who gives life has set you free from the law of sin and death. **3** For what the law was powerless to do because it was weakened by the flesh God did by sending his own Son in the likeness of sinful flesh to be a sin offering. And so he condemned sin in the flesh, **4** in order that the righteous requirement of the law might be fully met in us, who do not live according to the flesh but according to the Spirit.*

***5** Those who live according to the flesh have their minds set on what the flesh desires; but those who live in accordance with the Spirit have their minds set on what the Spirit desires. **6** The mind governed by the flesh is death, but the mind governed by the Spirit is life and peace. **7** The mind governed by the flesh is hostile to God; it does not submit to God's law, nor can it do so. **8** Those who are in the realm of the flesh cannot please God.*

9 You, however, are not in the realm of the flesh but are in the realm of the Spirit, if indeed the Spirit of God lives in you. And if anyone does not have the Spirit of Christ, they do not belong to Christ. 10 But if Christ is in you, then even though your body is subject to death because of sin, the Spirit gives life because of righteousness. 11 And if the Spirit of him who raised Jesus from the dead is living in you, he who raised Christ from the dead will also give life to your mortal bodies because of his Spirit who lives in you.

12 Therefore, brothers and sisters, we have an obligation—but it is not to the flesh, to live according to it. 13 For if you live according to the flesh, you will die; but if by the Spirit you put to death the misdeeds of the body, you will live.14 For those who are led by the Spirit of God are the children of God.

1. Circle the word "flesh" every time it appears in this passage.

2. Find all the circled words and write out everything we know about the flesh according to this passage:

_____

_____

_____

_____

_____

_____

_____

_____

3. Fill in the blanks from **Romans 8:6**

The mind governed by the flesh is _____ , but the mind governed by the Spirit is _____ and

_____ .

4. Fill in the blanks from **Romans 8:13**

For if you live according to the flesh, you will _____ ;
but if by the Spirit you _____ _____
_____ the misdeeds of the body, you will

_____ .

It is possible to have eternal life in Christ and still conduct ourselves in the flesh. When we do this—when we, as Christians, live according to our sinful nature as described in Romans 8—we will reap the consequences of our sin *in this life*. We will suffer loss, frustration, anxiety, confusion, etc. And all of this will eventually lead to death—relational death, emotional death, possibly even physical death. This is not to say that all bad things that happen to us are because of sinful choices *on our part*. (We addressed this in Lesson Five Discussion questions.) But we can be sure that sin always leads to death of some kind.

However, when we allow the Spirit to rule in our minds **(Rom 8:6)**, we will reap the consequences of this choice *in this life*—namely, by experiencing life and peace.

So, when dealing with the voice of the flesh or sinful nature DON'T

❀   Confuse the voice of the flesh with taking good care of our body

❀   Rebuke the flesh

❀   Give in to the flesh

What, then should we do? (Hint: We just read it in **Romans 8:13**)

We respond to the voice of the flesh by starving it, killing it, and crucifying it.

Wait. Didn't I just tell you to take good care of your body? And now I'm telling you to starve it, and kill it, and crucify it? Well, yes and no:

❀   Take good care of your physical body.

❀   Starve and crucify your sinful nature.

In your Bible, read **Galatians 5:13-25** and answer the following questions:

1. While we are called to be free, we are not to use our freedom to
_____ (v. 13).

2. According to verse 16, we should not gratify the deeds of the flesh. How does this verse say to accomplish this?

_____

3. According to verse 17, why can't we just do whatever we want to do?

_____

4. What are the works of the flesh?

_____

_____

_____

5. What is the fruit of the Spirit?

_____

_____

_____

6. Write out **Galatians 5:24** here word-for-word:

_____

_____

_____

Here is one of the few times in the Bible that "crucify" does not refer to the crucifixion of Jesus, but rather the way we are to approach the ongoing battle with our sinful desires. As you know, any living organism that is not fed will eventually die—exhibit A: All my houseplants. Living things can only last so long without food and water. This is also true of the sinful nature. If we deprive it, it will become weak and die.

In your Bible, read **Colossians 3**. We've already looked at a portion of this chapter when we discussed the peace of God in Lesson Six. But let's look at it now as it relates to the flesh.

1. According to **Colossians 3:2**, we are to set our minds on

_____ and not _____ .

2. Write out verse 5, word-for-word:

_____

_____

_____

3. Look at verses 8-9. What are the works of the flesh named here?

_____

_____

4. How do we deal with these?

_____

_____

According to Scripture, the only way to handle this sinful nature is to put it to death; that is, refuse to give it any of our time, attention, or energy. Do the opposite, even! Once you've identified that the voice in your head is the flesh/sinful nature, your job is to starve it until it dies.

That means...

When the voice inside you tells you that you can't get up early to pray because you deserve to sleep in, you get up and pray.

When the voice inside tells you that you have every right to be angry, you confess your anger to God and pray for the person who hurt you.

When the voice inside you tells you to say unkind words about your friend or coworker, you shut your mouth or say something kind instead.

When the voice inside says that you deserve recognition, you remind yourself that God will exalt you in due time, and then you humble yourself and serve someone.

When the voice inside says, "Explain yourself! Justify your actions! Write the longest text/email/social media post EVER!" you stop and remember God is your defender. Then you hit the delete button and walk away.

When the voice inside tells you to bend the truth just a little to get what you need, you choose to speak the truth in love and trust God to supply your needs.

When the voice inside tells you it's harmless to flirt with that married guy in the office, run in the other direction.

Crucifixion on a wooden cross was one of the most painful and degrading forms of execution. A person crucified in Jesus' day was first scourged or flogged until blood flowed. Shockingly, this was designed to hasten the death and lessen the ordeal. The victim was then forced to carry the crossbeam to the execution site, an act designed to shame the victim and break his will to live any longer. Then the victim was either tied or nailed to the beam. Eventually, death occurred by loss of blood circulation or coronary failure. If he was tied, the death could take days. Such executions were carried out in public places and the body was left to rot as birds came to degrade the body further.[38]

So, when Scripture tells us to "crucify the flesh," we can expect it to be hard, and ugly, and painful. We can expect it to take a while. We can expect our flesh to resist and rebel against our efforts. All of that is normal!

But also expect this: Every time you starve your sinful nature, it becomes weaker. The voice becomes fainter. What used to tempt you becomes dead to you and holds no power over you. The Spirit in you becomes stronger. The voice of God in you becomes clearer. When you live according to the Spirit, your new normal is Life and Peace.

> **A P P L Y**
>
> Go back to the "Pause and Listen" exercise at the beginning of this section. After every thought and subsequent action you identified as "the voice of the flesh," consider how you can apply what you've learned today. How can you respond to the voice of your flesh according to Scripture? What practical actions can you take to starve and crucify those specific thoughts? In the third column, write out a specific and doable response for each one and then write today's date. Then commit to put these new responses into practice today. At the end of this Bible study, I suggest you to come back to this page and see if that voice in your head is dead...or at least weaker from starvation.

SUMMARY

To respond to the Voice of the Flesh

Don't

* Confuse the voice of the flesh with taking good care of your body
* Rebuke the flesh
* Give in to the flesh

Do

* Starve, kill, crucify the flesh
* Expect the process to be difficult
* Expect yourself to become stronger

The Devil/Evil Spirits

Confession: Sometimes I don't want to say "yes" to God. Even when I know the yes means something good for me or for someone else. Because at some point between my yes and the fulfillment of my commitment, all hell will break loose in my life. This may not be everyone's experience, but with me this happens without fail, every single time. It has happened with every big yes I have ever said to God—every series I've taught at church, every Bible study I've written, every leadership position I've accepted, every major speaking engagement I've scheduled, and every child I've adopted into our family. It even happened with the current commitment to write this book. Which is unfortunate, because it has taken me almost a year to write it, which lends itself to a lot of hell-breaking-loose opportunities.

For years, I didn't understand what was happening. I didn't connect the dots between my obedience to God and the spiritual resistance that followed. I'm not one to blame every bad hair day, flat tire, and burnt piece of toast on the devil—that seems extreme (and also creepy) to me.

But the other extreme—and where I used to land most days—was concluding that this is just coincidence. It's just life. We live in a fallen world, and here's proof—it's called chaos. This irritability I'm battling? Menopause. This tension in my home? Sleep deprivation. This strife between my children? A developmental stage. This division between me and Jon? A season. This darkness I sense hovering over my family? Too much sugar.

You guys, it takes real discernment to be under spiritual attack and blame it on sugar.

The oppression you feel, the resistance you can't quite put your finger on, the chaos that seems to appear out of nowhere, the confusion that clutters your mind—consider that it may not be hormones or sleep deprivation or a season, but an outright spiritual attack. Whether you acknowledge it or not, you have a spiritual enemy who hates you. He is pure evil. **When you step out to seek God and obey His voice, the Enemy will try to stop you.**

I'm not trying to scare you—God has given us everything we need to be victorious against the Enemy (which we are going to study in a minute) so **we do not need to be afraid**. We do, however, need to be alert to the fact that the thoughts Satan sows into our mind are part of an overall spiritual attack against us. As the Apostle Paul said to the church in Corinth, we must not allow Satan to outwit us, for we are not ignorant of his schemes. (**2 Corinthians 2:11**)

What Does the Devil Sound Like?

In your Bible, find the passages below that describe the voice of Satan/evil. Then, write a brief description beside each one. You can choose from the phrases in the Word Bank below and add any of your own words. Many of the passages have more than one description that fits, and you can use the phrases from the Word Bank more than once. When you're finished, we are going to look at a few of these in greater depth.

Word Bank

Deception and lies contrary to God's word

Questioning God's goodness or intentions

Doubt, fear, discomfort ✓

Promising to give you something greater than what God will give you

Confusion, disorder, distraction, overwhelm ✓

Accusing and reminding you of past sins ✓

Lack of peace or a sense of restlessness, feeling pushed and pressured

Attacking your character or your value

Denial or discounting of the Lordship of Jesus Christ

Condemnation, guilt, ✓ *discouragement and shame*

Division and isolation from others, especially from the body of Christ

Genesis 3:1-5

_____

_____

Isaiah 48:22

_____

_____

Zechariah 3:1

_____

_____

Matthew 4:1-11

_____

_____

Mark 4:13-15

_____

_____

John 8:44

_____

_____

Romans 8:1

_____

_____

I Corinthians 12:12-27 (Satan's voice will be the opposite of what is described here)

_____

_____

I Corinthians 14:33

_____

_____

2 Timothy 1:7

_____

_____

I John 4:1-6

_____

_____

Revelation 12:10

_____

_____

Revelation 20:7-10

_____

_____

🔊 **Pause and Listen:** Did any of those descriptions jump out at you or surprise you? (Remember, when Scripture jumps out at you, pay attention. It may be God speaking to you.) Write them here as well as any thoughts you have.

_____

_____

_____

_____

_____

_____

_____

Deception and Lies Contrary to God's Word

People often ask me where I'm originally from. To be clear, nary a single person asked me that question until I was 28 years old and moved from Toledo, Ohio (my childhood home) to Jacksonville, Florida. My accent—particularly, the nasally short "a" sound as in "that cat is fantastic"—revealed that I was not raised in the Deep South but rather Northwest Ohio.

I've lost much of my Toledo accent since then. Yet, even now living in Louisville, Kentucky, almost 25 years after leaving my hometown, my speech patterns and pronunciations reveal that I am clearly not a Southern Belle.

I say "you guys" instead of "y'all." In fact, I would argue that "you guys" is a complete sentence.

I say my "I" with two syllables; as in, "*Ah-ee*'d like to eat that entire Derby *pah-ee*," (Yankee) instead of "*Ah*'d like to eat that entire Derby *Pah*" (Southern)

I pronounce "pin" and "pen" differently. Side note: Once on a spelling test, my youngest daughter received an error because the teacher said the word "pen," but it sounded to Elliana like "pin." So, of course, Elliana wrote "pin," not because she's a bad speller, but rather because we are aliens from a foreign northern land. The correct answer was "pen." I emailed the teacher to explain, but she didn't change the grade. Elliana cried because she didn't receive 100%.

And while I no longer say "pop" when referring to soft drinks, I have failed to adopt the Southern word "coke." Instead, I prefer the more universally accepted word, "soda," because I hate controversy of any kind—especially when inquiring about the available carbonated beverages at a restaurant.

Oh, and I say Louisville all wrong. According to reliable local sources, the following pronunciation variations are acceptable: *Luh-vul, Loo-a-vul,* or *Loo-a-ville.* Or, in the words of the ancient Louisvillian proverb: say it like you're drunk on bourbon. But to say, *Loo-ee-ville,* as I do, clearly pegs me as a Yankee.

When I first moved here, I was in the park, trying to make friends with a mom while our kids played together. She was discussing the upcoming birth of her newest baby and I asked her when she was due.

She said, "Derby Day."

To which I responded, "When is that?"

To which she responded first, by pausing for a good ten seconds and glaring at me through narrow eyes. And second, by saying in her sweet *Lul-vul* accent, "You're not from here, are you?"[39]

All that to say, accents reveal a person's place of origin.

Did you know that our enemy, Satan, also has an accent? No matter how hard the enemy tries, he can never sound exactly like God. He's got a native tongue, and God wants us to recognize it.

You read in **John 8:44** where Jesus called Satan a liar and the father of lies. Whenever someone is named the "father" of something, it means they are the originator, the founder, the creator, or the one with whom the "something" is most closely associated; as in, "Hippocrates is the Father of Modern Medicine" or "George Washington is the Father of the United States of America" or "Giorgio Moroder is the Father of Disco." (I had to look that last one up.)

Satan is the father of *lies*—the originator, the founder, the creator, and the one with whom lies are most closely associated. Lying is his native tongue, his original language. It's what he knows best. It's what he's been doing since the beginning of time and continues to do this very day. Even when he speaks truth, he twists it in order to deceive. He may try to sound like God, but his "lying accent" always gives him away. You can be sure whenever you hear a voice in your head twisting Scripture or speaking something contrary to God's word, this is the voice of Satan—*always*. The only way to discern the nuance of this accent is to hold the thought in question up to the Light of the written Word. (This is yet another reason why saturating your mind with Scripture is vital.)

But here's where it gets tricky: even if the thought is an exact quote from Scripture, it can still be Satan speaking it to you. Satan can twist the original purpose of the Scripture or pull a passage out of context and use it to question God's goodness or cause division within the Body of Christ. He can use God's word to drive fear into your heart or to confuse you about God's purpose for you. This is what cults do. This is also the very essence of legalism. They take the word of Life and skew it to become something burdensome, divisive, or downright abusive.

This is precisely what Satan tried to do to Jesus in **Matthew 4:6** when he quoted **Psalm 91:11-12** out of context to tempt Jesus to jump off a cliff. Let that sink in for a moment. Satan quoted the word of God *to the Word of God*. How much more do you think he will use this tactic on us, the Children of God?

Confusion, Disorder, Distraction, Overwhelm

Confusion is a subtle tactic of the enemy. Uncertainty is not always Satan. Distraction can happen when we forget to turn off phone notifications. Brain fog can happen after a night of fitful sleep. We all face ambiguous choices from time to time, and we won't always understand everything God leads us through—in fact, some things we won't understand until after we die. Confusion in life is normal.

But other times we experience confusion, distractions, or brain fog that comes directly from Satan.

In your Bibles, read **Ephesians 6:16** (we are going to study this passage in context later in this lesson). What kind of ammunition does the evil one throw at us?

_____

You guys. When Satan launches fire at you, he's not messing around. You can be certain his motive is to cause you serious harm or death—

he wants to destroy you. But other times Satan will not point the flaming arrow at you, but rather at something or someone you love—your kids, your marriage, your ministry, your work. He does this, not to destroy you, but *to distract you* from what God has called you to do. It's impossible to continue with God's work when your marriage is on fire. It's futile to tend to anything meaningful when your child is in crisis. This type of confusion or distraction is a classic satanic move and precisely why "all hell breaks loose" whenever you say yes to God.

If you feel a persistent brain-fog, an onslaught of racing thoughts, or a set of serious circumstances, which commence at the outset of your obedience to God and cause distraction from the call of God on your life, it is Satan.

In fact, I would venture to say that most of you are currently experiencing this type of attack as you work through this Bible study, am I right? Take heart, God has given us everything we need to quench this fiery attack. By the time you finish this lesson, you will be fully equipped for battle.

Denial of the Lordship of Christ

You read in **1 John 4:1-6** that every spirit that does not acknowledge Jesus is not from God. I always thought this one was kind of a no-brainer, like, of *course* if I'm tempted to deny Christ, it isn't God... *Duh!* Obviously. Sort of like the devil showing up with a red suit and a pitchfork. "I'm the Devil and I'm here to deny the Lordship of Christ."

But a rapidly growing trend is emerging where people—about one in five—describe themselves as "spiritual, but not religious."[40] Fed up with organized religion, they choose instead to seek spirituality through individualized practices like yoga, mediation, silence, solitude, and personal reflection. And listen, I understand that organized religion has had its problems—as much as I love my local church and the Church as a whole, I have problems with the way people have screwed it up, too. So, I understand why people may want to distance themselves from it. You may also recall, I'm the one who just taught you entire Bible study lessons on silence, solitude, and mediation. So, I'm not warning against those practices specifically. But we must be careful when our "spirituality" crosses the line from a life devoted to Jesus Christ into mysticism.

In your Bible, find **2 Timothy 3:1-5** and fill in the blanks below. (This is NIV.)

But mark this: There will be terrible times in the last days. **2** People will be _____ , lovers of money, boastful, proud, abusive, disobedient to their parents, ungrateful, unholy, **3** without love, unforgiving, slanderous, without self-control, brutal, not lovers of the good, **4** treacherous, rash, conceited, lovers of _____ rather than lovers of _____ **5** having a _____ but _____ . Have nothing to do with such people.

This is a letter written by the Apostle Paul to his disciple, Timothy, regarding the last days. The "last days" not only referred to the day in which they were living at the time, but also the days just before the return of Christ—*the days in which we are now living.*

Paul describes a list of dreadful behaviors—abusive, ungrateful, unholy, etc.—and then tacked onto the end of that list something equally dreadful: having a form of godliness, but denying the power thereof. In other words, an appearance of devotion and piety towards God, but rejecting God Himself. This is precisely what we see today—a "spiritual life" without submitting to the Holy Spirit.

In this post-modern cultural shift, it is acceptable and encouraged to practice your faith (a form of godliness and spirituality)—valuing the freedom to define your own spirituality is one of the main characteristics of this group of people. But not if you define your spirituality by belief in Jesus Christ.

Believing in God is popular.

Believing that *Jesus Christ is the Son of God and the only way to salvation* is not popular.

Praying to God *in your own way*: acceptable.

Praying to God *in Jesus' name*: unacceptable.

Searching *inside yourself for truth and beauty*: encouraged.

Searching *the words of Jesus for truth and beauty*: discouraged.

In fact, the name of Jesus is downright offensive to the general public. "God" is not offensive. But "Jesus" is offensive. Isn't that strange?

The "spiritual, but not religious group" also has a non-traditional and unorthodox definition of God. God can be a "being," "a state of mind," "a power," or just "a presence." They will say things like, "I believe in God. I choose to call it 'God,' but you may call it something different...." Many of them refer to God as "he or she." Defining God in your own way is very important to them.

This type of mindset is seeping into the Church, as well. Many contemporary female Christian writers and speakers straddle this line. Just yesterday I was listening to two of the most popular Christian women today—both of them New York Times best-selling authors, both of them with hundreds of thousands of followers, and both of them writers I have followed for a decade—talking about truth and beauty. They both, through tears, recounted how they found "real truth and beauty" by rejecting the "lies" they had been told in church. They declared that Eve was not wrong for wanting more than what God offered her in the Garden, and we as women are not wrong for wanting more today. They encouraged listeners to "look deep within" and "trust their instincts" and "chase everything they want." They spent 60 minutes telling women that we should shed the oppressive definitions of God and Christianity taught to us in church, and embrace and explore our true desires. They claimed that true freedom and world change would only come when women learn to chase our inner truth.

And I was over here, like, okaaaay... *What?* I was trying so hard to follow their logic and grasp onto something substantial. It just sounded like the centuries-old gospel of humanism mixed with feminism then camouflaged in inspiration— where the goal and the god is Self. Where does that lead, really? Because, I'm just being honest, if I look for answers deep within myself and chase everything I want apart from Jesus, it will lead me straight to my warm bed with my soft blankie, a book, and a tub of peanut butter chocolate fudge ice-cream. I agree that women all over the globe currently live under oppression, and I agree that the church has not always done a great job of representing Christ and Truth to women (or to men, for that matter), but I completely disagree that true freedom is found in chasing Self or in seeking spirituality apart from Jesus.

In your Bible, read **2 Corinthians 11:12-15**. What does this passage say about Satan? What does it say about Satan's servants?

_____

_____

_____

Hear me: I'm not suggesting that these Christian writers or speakers are Satan's servants! What I am suggesting is that Satan is cunning and insidious and clever and shrewd. I'm suggesting that he is trying to work his way into our doctrines and theology and undermine the authority of Jesus Christ. I'm suggesting that the way he does this is not by screaming at us as we innocently walk by his evil picket line, but rather by subtly presenting options to us that appear to be loving and inclusive and unifying.

But make no mistake. His motives are never to unify. His motives are never love. His endgame is always deception, distraction, destruction, and death. Be on guard.

🔊 **Pause and Listen:** Look back over the descriptions of Satan's voice that we studied. Take a few minutes right now to ask God to reveal to you the specific thoughts that come into your mind which originate with Satan. Write everything God is revealing to you here:

_____

_____

_____

_____

_____

_____

_____

_____

_____

_____

_____

_____

How to Respond to the Voice of Satan

Just like the voice of the flesh, some strategies work with Satan and some don't. When my kids were little, they'd say things like, "Satan is just a big poopy head." I'd agree that Satan is, in fact, the biggest poopy head in the whole universe of poopy heads. But calling him a poopy head will not make him leave us alone. So, let's first talk about what does not work (i.e., calling him "poopy head") when we are responding to the devil.

When Responding to the Voice of Satan, Don't

1. Argue with reason and logic. Back when social media was new and I had religious zeal for days, I thought I could change the world with common sense and rationale. Given adequate time and a platform to clearly state my position, I was convinced I could persuade anyone to my side. Have you ever gotten into a heated debate with someone over a controversial issue on social media? Yeah. If you have, you know how this story ends. Arguing on social media is absolutely futile. It's like trying to cuddle a feral cat. You're all, "here kitty, kitty, I have tuna for you," and the cat hisses and lunges at your face. Logic and reason check out on the Facebook login page—just ask anyone who tried to calmly debate politics in the 2016 presidential election…or the 2020 presidential election.

It's the same with Satan (and Twitter). Don't argue with evil. Don't debate the devil. Satan has been studying humanity since the beginning of time and has been studying you—your responses and your weaknesses—your entire life. His attacks are strategic, specific, and tailor-made for you. He is not interested in logic and reason. He will never be persuaded by your well-crafted and thoughtful responses.

2. Plead ignorance. Pretending Satan doesn't exist will not cause him to evaporate. Besides, after working though this lesson, you already know too much to ignore him. (Sorry/not sorry.)

3. Respond or react in your own strength, apart from God. For about 10 years, we lived in a pretty little neighborhood on the outskirts of Louisville. Our street was teeming with children (including mine) who played outside all day long. I felt completely comfortable allowing my children to play outside without my constant supervision, most of the time. It was a very safe neighborhood overall, except for one thing— The Speeders.

Our neighborhood had a main road—a giant circle about a mile around, with a speed limit of 25 mph—which is where our house was located. At 25 mph, cars could safely navigate the roads while children did what children sometimes do: accidentally kick balls in the road and chase after them. The problem was that on that entire mile-long main drag was only one stop sign. One! In other words, despite the safe speed limit, it was more like a NASCAR speedway than it was a kid-friendly neighborhood.

So, sometimes when it was nice outside, I would stand in the driveway and supervise the safety of the kids while talking with our neighbors. Our conversations would usually go something like this:

Me: Hey! How are you guys? Wow, your flowerbeds look fantastic! How is Kate enjoying kindergarten? SLOW DOWN!!!!!!!!!!!!

Neighbor: Thanks. Kate loves kindergarten. Oh, and I've got some tomato plants in pots in the back. I'll give you a few when they are ready. SLOW DOWN!!!!!!!!!!!!!!!!!!!!!!

Me: Oh wow, thank you. I can't wait. Homegrown tomatoes are my favorite. SLOW DOWN!!!!!!!!!

And we'd carry on like this, alternating between friendly chitchat and frantic screaming, never missing a beat. Sometimes when a car was going particularly fast, all the parents and the children would shout SLOW DOWN in unison, waving our arms like the neighborhood was on fire. We even tried placing those yellow plastic signs in the street that read "Slow Children Playing." Sometimes, we'd literally stand in the street, trying to block the cars like a human barrier.

Even though we were right and justified in our concern for our children, and even though we were speaking words that are true and accurate, our spontaneous screaming and flailing made little difference in the speeding problem. Every once in a while, a driver would hear us and slow down. But most drivers either ignored us or they revved their engine in rebellion. Occasionally, an agitated driver would flip us a hand gesture. #classy

Then once or twice a year, a police officer would show up. He'd come unannounced and quietly park on a side street a few houses up from us. He never shouted. He never screamed. He never flailed. He just sat and waited for cars to drive past him, exceeding the speed limit.

The cars that saw him? They slowed down immediately. The cop didn't even need to turn on his lights or siren or anything. The mere sight of him caused The Speeders to slow to a crawl past our house. It was a thing of beauty. The unfortunate drivers who failed to see the officer? Well, they got the blue flashing light and a speeding ticket. A thing of greater beauty.

Both the police officer and the parents had the same goal—slowing down The Speeders to protect the children. One was effective. One was not. What was the difference between the officer and the parents?

The difference was in the officer's authority.

See, that police officer's uniform, his badge, his car—they said, "I represent something bigger than me. I come in the name of the Louisville Metro Police Department. And that entity has the ability to administer punishment if you do not obey the law. Punishment by way of a fine, a court date, and potential jail time."

So, when you encounter your enemy, Satan, you can scream and cry and flail and berate him all you want. You can even scream Scripture at him. And if you do not clothe yourself with God's authority, he will drive right by you, flip you off, and rev his engine. All. Day. Long. It's like me in my yoga pants trying to catch The Speeders.

But when you show up in your uniform, you say to Satan, "I represent something bigger than me. I come in the name of Jesus Christ, the Living God. All authority in heaven and earth belongs to Him. And He has the power over you and over death, hell, and the grave. In Jesus' Name, I command you to STOP!"

The armor of God is your uniform. It speaks for you, and the enemy must stop when you resist him while you are wearing your spiritual armor.

Remember when we said early in this lesson that rebuking the flesh is not an effective strategy? Well, here is where rebuking *will* work: We can rebuke Satan when we come in the name and under the authority of Jesus Christ.

That's the difference between what does not work and what does work. So, with that, let's talk about how to put on our uniform and suit up with the authority of Jesus.

When Responding to the Voice of Satan, Do

To provide an outline on how to respond to spiritual opposition and the taunting of Satan, we are going to take a look at **Nehemiah chapter 4**.

Go ahead and turn there in you Bible. But before we dive in, let me offer some background.

The Babylonians conquered Judah in 586 BC. Persia, in turn, conquered Babylon in 539 BC, and shortly thereafter they allowed the Jews to return to Jerusalem. Despite opposition, the returned exiles came back in three groups:

- Zerubbabel led the first return and rebuilt the temple.

- Ezra led the second group and rebuilt the people.

- A third group, led by Nehemiah, returned and rebuilt Jerusalem's wall.

This is where we are in Nehemiah 4—The challenges of rebuilding their homeland had demoralized the Jews, and the wall of Jerusalem remained in rubble. Now, it's about 444 BC and Nehemiah is leading the Israelites to rebuild the wall around Jerusalem. We enter the story where the work has actually begun and the Israelites are being incessantly mocked and threatened by their enemies.

Now read **Nehemiah 4** in your Bible and answer the questions below.

1. What is the first thing Nehemiah did in response to the opposition? (vv. 4-5)?

_____

_____

Put a bookmark in **Nehemiah 4** while we look at a related scripture. In your Bibles, read **Ephesians 6:10-18** describing the armor of God and write verse 18 word-for-word:

_____

_____

_____

Put another bookmark in **Ephesians 6** (we're coming back to this), and turn to **Mark 9:14-29**. Why couldn't the disciples drive the evil spirit out of the boy?

_____

I hate to give you the answers to these questions or insult your intelligence, but I don't want you to miss this: **The most important response to a spiritual attack is always prayer.** It was the first thing Nehemiah did. It was the last thing Paul mentioned when he described our spiritual armor. And it was the one thing lacking when disciples failed to drive out the evil spirit from the boy. **Prayer. Prayer. Prayer.** In fact, in some cases, prayer alone is not enough to drive out the enemy.

Sometimes we see spiritual battles fought with extended periods of prayer coupled with fasting (Remember **Daniel 10**?)

2. Back to Nehemiah, what did Nehemiah and the workers do in the face of opposition in verses 6 and 15? Circle the correct answer:

A) Ran and hid

B) Posted a long Facebook rant

C) Screamed insults back at their enemies

D) Vowed never to obey the Lord again because it's too hard

E) Continued working with all their heart

Don't you love how even though the enemies kept taunting and threatening them, and even though they were exhausted and scared, they just kept working? We must do the same. Listen, your enemy will threaten you. This isn't time to whine and complain and vent. This isn't the time to cower and say, "I'm never gonna say yes to God's plan for me again. Every time I do, things go bad." Yes, of course they do. We've established this. This is a war we are in, after all. Now, **get back to work.**

REFLECT AND ASSESS

Have you been tempted to quit a project, a mission, or a ministry because of the strong spiritual opposition? Explain:

_____

_____

If you are feeling this way now, pray and ask God to give you the perseverance to keep working. Write a short prayer here:

_____

_____

_____

3. Fill in the blank for **Nehemiah 4:13-14** below:

13 *Therefore I stationed some of the people behind the lowest points of the wall at the exposed places, posting them by _____,* *with their swords, spears and bows.* **14** *After I looked things over, I stood up and said to the nobles, the officials and the rest of the people, "Don't be afraid of them. Remember the Lord, who is great and awesome, and fight for your _____ , your _____ and your _____ , your _____ and your _____ ."*

Now, in your Bibles flip back to **Ephesians 6**. According to verse 12...

Our struggle is not against what?

_____

But is against what?

_____

_____

When you are under spiritual attack, Satan will want you to blame everyone but him—blame your spouse, blame your kids, blame your pastor, blame yourself, blame sugar—whatever. That's why he often aims his flaming arrows at your family.

When you see a cherished relationship going up in flames, it's tempting to panic and go over and smother that thing or beat it with a wet towel. It's tempting to get angry at the very thing or person under attack because they are freaking out, forgetting that they are under spiritual attack, as well! I am so guilty of this—especially when it's my child. **You have got to recognize who your real enemy is so you can fight the right one.** Don't fight your family, fight for your family!

REFLECT AND ASSESS **Where have you been fighting a person when you needed to be fighting your spiritual enemy?**

_____

_____

_____

4. Back to **Nehemiah 4**, what did Nehemiah and the Jews start doing differently beginning in verse 16?

_____

_____

Satan loves when we are isolated. When we are alone, he can feed us lies, and no one is there to say, "Hey! That's not God!" This is why we must stay connected to other believers—we need people to watch our backs. Depending on your season of life, your temperament, or you level of busyness you may or may not even know who to ask to join you in prayer during a spiritual attack. That's a weird request if you aren't particularly close to someone. Personally, I have had seasons where I was involved in a fantastic Bible study or a small group, or had a close Christian girlfriend I knew I could call any time, night or day, and it wouldn't be weird. But other times—especially during the baby years of parenting, the busy middle school years of activity, or immediately following a relocation—I've been isolated. These are times when we must be deliberate and strategic. Disconnection means vulnerability. This is Satan's favorite time to pull us aside and whisper in our ear...

Is that really what God said?

Who do you think you are?

This is all too much.

Nobody cares about you.

You'll never change.

You've messed this up too many times.

You're horrible.

You're hopeless.

You're too much.

You're not enough.

I Peter 5:8-9 *says, "Be alert and of sober mind. Your enemy the devil prowls around like a roaring lion looking for someone to devour. Resist him, standing firm in the faith, because you know that the family of believers throughout the world is undergoing the same kind of sufferings."*

One of the most effective ways to resist the devil and stand firm in the faith is to join together with others. Next time you feel vulnerable to spiritual attack, gather your people. Be strategic. Be calculated. This is not the time to go it alone. Find some prayer partners to watch your back while you work. Be direct. Tell them plainly, "I'm doing some important work for God and I am under a spiritual attack. I need you to pray for me."

REFLECT AND ASSESS

What thoughts do you have repeatedly that you now suspect as the voice of the enemy?

_____

_____

_____

_____

A
P
P
L
Y

Who can you call the next time you need someone to watch your back while you work for God? Write the name(s) here:

_____

_____

Can you reach out to them today and ask them to partner with you in prayer against the voices in your mind or against the spiritual attack on something or someone you love?

_____

_____

5. **Nehemiah** 4:17-23 gives a stunning word picture of what we must do with our weapons while we work. Describe what is happening here in your own words:

_____

_____

The important lesson here is to never, ever drop your weapons. Whether you're working or going to get water, you keep that weapon at-the-ready so you are always prepared to fight the enemy when he attacks.

Let's look one more time at **Ephesians 6:10-18**, and answer the questions below, to identify each piece of our armor as well as our weapons.[41] For most of you, this will be familiar, but it's a good refresher.

First, why do we put on the armor of God (vv. 11, 13)?

_____

What are the pieces of the armor?

The belt of _____

The breastplate of _____

The shoes of the gospel of _____

The shield of _____

The helmet of _____

The sword of the _____, which is
the _____

Now, turn to **James 4:7** and write it here, word-for-word:

_____

_____

Read **Matthew 4:1-11**

Here Jesus demonstrates for us exactly how to resist the devil by using the word of God. This passage begins by telling us that Jesus was led by the spirit into the wilderness **to be tempted by the devil**. With every temptation, what did Jesus say in response (vv. 4, 7, 10)?

_____

Notice in verse 10, Jesus offered a firm rebuke, and with that, the devil left Him. This underscores once again the importance of knowing the Word of God. Even Jesus Himself quoted the word of God to resist the devil. He is our example. This is how we exercise our authority.

One more passage before we wrap up this section. Turn to **Revelation 12:10-12**. This passage describes two weapons in our arsenal that defeat our adversary, the Devil. What are they? (v. 11)

_____

_____

SUMMARY

To Respond to the Voice of Satan...

Don't

* Be afraid
* Argue with reason and logic
* Plead ignorance
* Respond or react in your own strength apart from God

Do

* Pray and fast
* Continue the work of God
* Fight the enemy, not people
* Gather people to fight the spiritual battle with you
* Put on the full armor of God

❋   Keep your weapons ready at all times

❋   Resist the Devil with the Word of God

❋   Rebuke the Devil with the authority of Jesus Christ

🔊 **Pause and Listen:** What strategies are jumping out at you right now? What Scriptures do you feel particularly drawn to? Is anything you read in this lesson so far surprising to you? Ask God to reveal to you where you should focus your attention as you move forward. Write what you hear God saying to you:

_____

_____

_____

_____

_____

_____

Four Final Thoughts on The Voice of the Enemy

In your Bible read **Matthew 16:13-28**

My heart goes out to Peter every time I read this story. I mean, consider that Peter had been hand-selected by the Messiah, not only to be one of the twelve apostles, but also to be one of His closest friends— His *inner circle*. Peter left everything he knew to follow Him. He walked with Jesus and sat under His teaching, day in and day out for three years. If any human being had a front row seat to the grit and glory of Jesus' ministry, it was Peter. When Jesus asked, *"Who do you say that I am?"* Peter was the only one who answered the question correctly. Jesus, Himself, affirmed Peter in front of all the apostles by declaring that the Father in Heaven had bestowed upon him special revelation. And then Jesus handed Peter the keys to the Kingdom of Heaven!

Things were looking fantastic for Peter and his future ministry.

But then, in the very next conversation, Jesus begins to explain to Peter and the other disciples how He must suffer many things—die, even—and then be raised to life again.

I can totally see Peter in all his misplaced zeal: *What? Die!? How can that be? Jesus can't die. I love Jesus. I would give my life for Him in a heartbeat. I absolutely refuse to receive this negative confession, even if Jesus Himself is saying it.*

And in all his "special discernment into spiritual things" (Jesus told him he had it!), he decides it was time to pull Jesus aside and counsel Him a little. After all, he did, in fact, hold the keys to the kingdom. Whatever he bound on earth would be bound in Heaven.

Right?

"Peter took him aside and began to rebuke him. 'Never, Lord!' he said. 'This shall never happen to you!'"

Wrong.

"Jesus turned and said to Peter, 'Get behind me, Satan! You are a stumbling block to me; you do not have in mind the things of God, but the things of men.'"

Jesus doesn't simply correct Peter. No. Jesus rebukes him, calls him Satan, declares him a stumbling block, and accuses him of not having in mind the things of God, but the things of men.

Ouch.

The Bible doesn't tell us what Peter said or did in response, but if it were me, I would have busted into tears. I want to cry now just reading it. Can you imagine the humiliation and confusion Peter must have felt at that moment? For a long time I didn't understand why Jesus was so harsh with Peter. I mean, Peter was literally one of Jesus' closest friends. Of course Peter did not like the idea of Jesus dying. That only seems reasonable of a close friend to argue about this. Why in the world, then did Jesus rebuke Peter and call him Satan?

Before we answer that, let me tell you the first thing we learn from this passage about the voice of Satan:

1. Satan can speak through any person. Even people who love you. Even well-meaning people who don't want to see you suffer. Even people who have heard God clearly on your behalf in the past.

In the Introduction, I shared the story of young Jon and Sandy seeking our pastor's blessing as we prepared to move from our hometown and relocate to a new city. Leaving our church was one of the many things I dreaded about this move. This was the church I loved. The church where much of my family attended. The church where Jon and I dedicated our hearts to God, got baptized, and got married.

Up until that point in my life, deciding if we should move was the most difficult decision I had ever made. We did not take it lightly, by any stretch of the imagination. Over the course of months, we fasted, prayed, sought godly counsel, and prayed some more. The more we sought God, the clearer it became to us that God was leading us to relocate.

And yet, **during that time, some of the most difficult conversations I had were with people who loved me the most.** People who loved God. People who had spoken God's will to me in the past. People who didn't want to see Jon and me make a huge mistake. Some of those conversations were downright confrontational. Several people warned us that we were leaving God's protection. They questioned our motives, our heart-condition, and our salvation. Some people predicted that if we left our particular church or our denomination, we would fall away from God completely.

This was all painful, lonely, and confusing.

While I totally understood and appreciated their concern for our spiritual health, they were wrong. Sincere, but wrong. Just like Peter to Jesus, **they were speaking the exact opposite of God's will for our lives.** You'll be relieved to know I didn't call any of them Satan. (Well, not to their faces.) But I certainly did a lot of rebuking in my private prayer time.

Be on guard even with those who love God and love you. Hold everything anyone says to you against the Word of God, against what you know to be the truth, and against what you know God is speaking to your heart. It's too easy for people's love and concern for you to eclipse their spiritual discernment, especially when an option you are considering adversely affects their lives.

2. Be aware of how Satan has spoken to you or tempted you in the past. I think one reason Jesus was so direct with Peter was that Jesus clearly remembered a similar conversation He had with Satan in the desert after His 40-day fast. (**Matthew 4**) Satan tried to convince Jesus that He could achieve greatness without suffering. But Jesus knew the word of God. He understood His mission. He knew He was the Sacrificial Lamb. Without the shedding of His blood, there would be no remission of sins.

Though Peter's words sounded innocent—even noble and valiant and righteous—they were anything but. What Peter was suggesting was in direct opposition to God's plan. If Peter had had his way, his salvation and the salvation of the entire world would have been compromised.

That's huge.

Obviously, nothing we will ever decide will be of the same magnitude of Jesus' death on the cross. But as you seek to discern the voices in your head, consider how you know Satan has lied to you or accused you in the past. During one very difficult season in our family, at the climax of a giant argument, one of my loved ones looked me in the eye and said, "You spend all that time praying and reading the Bible and it's not changing you. Nothing will ever change you. It's not working and it will never work."

I've had some pretty awful things spoken to me in my life, but nothing has ever sounded more evil to me than those words at that moment. They matched verbatim the voice I heard in my head daily. This was a season where I was struggling on every level—in my parenting, my ministry, my marriage, my identity, my worth—everything was confusing and shaky and crumbling. I was seeking God in a way I had never done prior, trying to change the situation—but mostly trying to change me. But as I pressed in, I fought a daily battle against thoughts that the situation was hopeless, I was hopeless, and no amount of prayer or Bible reading would ever make a difference. The accusation that came out of my loved one's mouth gave a human voice to the thoughts I already had. I knew exactly where the words originated—not with my loved one, but with my adversary, the Devil.

And so, rather than fighting against my loved one, I rebuked and resisted my real enemy. I refused to respond to this person, and instead, I fought a spiritual battle with spiritual weapons. I knew to do this because I recognized the voice speaking to me originated not from the heart of this person, but from spiritual wickedness in the heavenly realm. Just like Peter, this person had no idea Satan was speaking through them.

3. Satan's voice often appeals to the flesh. Therefore, discerning between Satan and your flesh can get blurry. Again, looking back at **Matthew 4** where Satan tempted Jesus, he tempted Him with food, power, and kingdoms. All of these things appealed to Jesus' flesh. Satan did the same thing when he tempted Eve in the garden when he appealed to her desire for knowledge. (**Genesis 3:5**) This makes perfect sense, if you consider it would not technically be "tempting" to us if it were not appealing to our flesh in some way (pride, material wealth, recognition, sexual desire, etc.)

In times like this, we mustn't get too hung up on who's saying what (is this my flesh or the devil?). Like all things in life (except for math, maybe) there are no hard and fast rules about which voice is the flesh and which voice is Satan. It's all messy and overlapping, so don't make yourself crazy with trying to figure out if you should rebuke it or starve it or whatever. Remember the most important thing is to know the Truth. Then we'll be able to recognize the other voices as "not God," no matter who they are or what they are saying, and you can safely ignore them. If you need to fight a spiritual battle, trust God to reveal that to you.

4. If you still aren't sure who is speaking (God, your flesh, or the Devil), just wait and continue to seek God. Obviously, some decisions must be made within a certain time frame—job opportunities, purchase and sale of homes, college choices, relationships. But rest assured, God knows all of that. Don't worry, and don't feel pressured to make a big move in the name of missed opportunity. If you truly don't know if God is telling you to move forward, and especially if you are hearing conflicting voices, **don't do anything.**

I firmly believe God is more concerned with the condition of our hearts than He is with the particulars of any decision we make. He is more concerned with the refining our faith than He is with the house we live in. He is more concerned with the conforming of our character than He is with the job we take. His main goal for our lives is to draw us closer to Him so we can lead others to Him.

And besides, God specializes in do-overs. If you miss an opportunity because, out of a pure and sincere heart, you failed to act upon it, then I trust He will use that missed opportunity for your good. I also believe God is able to create new and better opportunities for the pure-hearted. He's not confined by the same human restrictions we are. He sees everything from a perfect perspective. He owns everything. He controls everything. He is sovereign over everything. He is certainly able to work with a pure-hearted follower whose heart's desire is to hear and obey the voice of the Good Shepherd—the humble servant who doesn't want to follow the wrong voice.

A P P L Y

Whenever I sense a strong attack from Satan, my very first line of defense is to get alone with God, turn on worship music, and sing. Then I write out scripture-based prayers and pray them out loud, with my actual voice. When I do these things, it ushers in instant clarity. Write down a detailed strategy you can take the next time you are bombarded with voices that are "not God."

_____

_____

_____

_____

_____

FOR DISCUSSION

- Have you encountered the "spiritual but not religious" mindset in culture? Where have you seen it? How have you responded to it? Would you describe yourself this way? Why or why not?

_____

_____

_____

_____

_____

_____

_____

_____

_____

_____

_____

_____

_____

_____

_____

_____

_____

_____

_____

✿ Women have suffered oppression throughout history and continue to suffer today. As women, discuss how we might simultaneously hold the messages of freedom and equality and world-change, while also holding the messages of death-to-self and submission to Christ. Discuss how one does not negate the other.

_____

_____

_____

_____

_____

_____

_____

_____

_____

_____

_____

_____

_____

_____

_____

_____

_____

❀ Can you recall a time where you missed a God-given opportunity, but God provided a Plan B or a complete do-over? Share this with your group.

_____

_____

_____

_____

_____

_____

_____

_____

_____

_____

_____

_____

_____

_____

_____

_____

_____

_____

_____

✿   What is your biggest takeaway from this lesson?

_____

_____

_____

_____

_____

_____

_____

_____

_____

_____

_____

_____

_____

_____

_____

_____

_____

_____

_____

NOTES

_____

_____

_____

_____

_____

_____

_____

_____

_____

_____

_____

_____

_____

_____

_____

_____

_____

_____

_____

Lesson Eight

When God Speaks Through Other People

PROPHECY IN THE OLD AND NEW TESTAMENTS

"Now the Berean Jews were of more noble character than those in Thessalonica, for they received the message with great eagerness and examined the Scriptures every day to see if what Paul said was true."

ACTS 17:11

I woke up that hot, muggy morning in May much like every other morning, with a fresh cup of coffee and my computer. As I opened my email inbox, I was delighted to see a message from my friend Jean:

Dear Sandy,

I woke up in the middle of the night with this scripture on my mind. God told me to send it to you. Psalm 121.

I lift up my eyes to the hills—where does my help come from? My help comes from the LORD, the Maker of heaven and earth. He will not let your foot slip—he who watches over you will not slumber; indeed, he who watches over Israel will neither slumber nor sleep. The LORD watches over you—the LORD is your shade at your right hand; the sun will not harm you by day, nor the moon by night. The LORD will keep you from all harm—he will watch over your life; the LORD will watch over your coming and going both now and forevermore.

I'm praying for you!
Love, Jean

Over the next few weeks, that scripture would prove to sustain me. We were in the process of moving from our home in Florida and relocating to Kentucky. We lived in Florida for eight years, and we loved it. I mean, we *loved it-loved it*. Everything about it, really. We solidified our marriage while living there. My son Noah was born and died while living there. My children Rebekah and Elijah were born there. I had great friends, great neighbors, and a thriving ministry in a warm and welcoming church. We had spent eight years enjoying the Florida sunshine while living only 20 minutes from the beach. (I have mentioned a time or ten how much I love the beach.) But, alas, Jon was starting a new job, which meant we were pulling up our tender Florida roots and moving to Kentucky, where the nearest ocean was…uh…*in Florida.*

Every visit with friends was for the sole purpose of savoring the final moments before saying goodbye. And every other minute of every day was designated to packing up and tying up loose ends. My house barely resembled the home I had worked so hard to build. It was the "fake house" we showed to the prospective buyers; that is, the house with no appliances on the counter tops, no toys on the floor, and no food in the oven. Instead, we had freshly painted neutral walls, burning scented candles, and smooth jazz playing in the background. (No one lives like this. Especially not those of us with small kids.)

Moving to Kentucky meant my husband would have the job of his dreams. But for me, it meant starting over: new house, new friends, new neighbors, new church, new doctors, and worst of all—NEW HAIR DRESSER!!!!! (I paid dearly for this move in the form of bad hair for the first two years we lived here, thanks to an inexperienced colorist—I call it, "The Hair-Frying of 2005".)

So, on that hot morning in May, before I began the craziness of strapping my two-year-old and my four-year-old into the car seat so I could create the "fake house," and drive them around the neighborhood while strangers decided if they liked or disliked my floor plan, I meditated on the verse my dear friend sent me. Every single word jumped out at me. Every. Single. Word. I was so thankful for a God who would send a message to me at the perfect time—a friend who was sensitive enough to hear God's voice on my behalf.

I read and reread that precious Psalm. Over the next two months, it became my daily bread. Though the flurry of May and June often left me emotionally and physically drained, I stood on God's promise— trusting God knew where we were and where we were going, trusting that He'd keep us from all harm, and trusting that He'd not let our feet slip. Through the truth of God's word, I found strength to do what I had to do: say goodbye to everything I loved and trust God in our new city.

Before long, we were driving away from our Florida home and heading north.

Yeehaw.

After settling into our new house, one of our first priorities was finding a church. With a toddler and a preschooler whose worlds had been turned upside-down, this task proved more difficult than I had anticipated. Week-by-week, I peeled my screaming babies off me to place them in yet, another unfamiliar childcare situation with more strangers, more change, and more transition. Meanwhile, Jon and I tried to make a snapshot decision whether this would be our new church-family. All I wanted to do was establish some roots, find some friends, and connect with some families. But even that was proving to be emotionally and physically draining.

One Sunday morning, I reached my limit. The kids were crying. I was crying. And I found myself seething in the back row of another strange, new church with a whimpering toddler on my lap, wondering what the heck God was thinking when He told us to move from beautiful, comfortable Florida to strange, uncomfortable Kentucky. I just wanted to go home—*to our Florida home*. Just about then, the pastor interrupted the worship service to address the congregation.

"Sorry," he began as he approached the podium, *"You know I don't usually do this, but this scripture is really on my heart, and I feel like there is someone here who needs to hear it."*

Then he opened up his Bible and began reading:

I lift up my eyes to the hills— where does my help come from? My help comes from the LORD, the Maker of heaven and earth. He will not let your foot slip— he who watches over you will not slumber; indeed, he who watches over Israel will neither slumber nor sleep. The LORD watches over you—the LORD is your shade at your right hand; the sun will not harm you by day, nor the moon by night. The LORD will keep you from all harm—he will watch over your life; the LORD will watch over your coming and going both now and forevermore.

The church we visited that day became our new church home, and continues to be after nearly 16 years. The pastor who heard God's voice and spoke what he heard that day was Tim—the man who would come to be my pastor, my boss, and one of my most cherished friends.

This moment was pivotal for us in deciding where to put down our roots, because, as you have probably gathered from everything you've read so far, sitting under a pastor who hears the voice of God was (and is) vital to me. Not only that, but sitting under a pastor who will hear the voice of God *on my behalf* and then speak it to me was a benefit I didn't even know I wanted. We had come full circle.

Rewind eight years prior...

I have to admit, after the incident in the back of the church in Toledo where my pastor and my husband both claimed to know God's will for me before making the move to Florida, (I just realized that God speaks a lot to me in the backs of churches!) I became very skeptical of all people who said they heard God's voice on my behalf. In the churches I've attended the last 30 years, it is very normal for people to say, "I feel like God is saying to you…" or "I have a 'word' for you." When I first began to experience this, it was both wonderful and scary. When the "word" was from God, it was awesome! When the "word" was not, I was confused and fearful: *Did God really say that? What does it mean? What am I supposed to do now?*

Because I lacked spiritual maturity, sometimes people would speak something to me, and I worried for days. One time, a person walked right up to me while I was working with the babies in the church nursery and said, "God says He's going to test you and Jon in your finances."

What the heck does THAT mean? Jon had lost his job the year prior and we were without work for six months. We were still recovering emotionally and financially from that, so I was immediately fearful it would happen again. (That "prophecy" never came to pass, by the way.)

One time we gave a large amount of money toward a well-known ministry because the evangelist promised God would bless us "tenfold" and pay off our house. (We did eventually pay off our house, but it was more than a decade later, and it was because God gave us wisdom and self-discipline to stick to a budget and pay extra on the principal, not because of some supernatural financial miracle after a "sacrificial gift.")

Other times, I wrestled with the inconsistency between what a person said to me and what I thought God was speaking to my own heart—especially in the early days of parenting, where unsolicited "prophetic parenting advice" was the norm about everything from feeding schedules to discipline to how often I should hold my new baby.

It was all very confusing when people came at me with "God said this" and "God said that," because none of these people who spoke to me were outwardly deceptive or mean-spirited. In fact, in most cases, they were reputable Christians with a sincere desire to speak what they thought God was saying. Some were a little more direct than others, but I never sensed any of them were insincere or manipulative—except maybe the evangelist who promised God would pay off our house after we wrote him a large check for his ministry.

After being cornered one too many times, I started to avoid certain people altogether. Seriously, if I saw them approaching me, I would do an about-face. The fact that they were allowed to freely walk about cornering unsuspecting members of the Body with "I have a 'word' for you" troubled me tremendously. Why was no one holding them accountable?

It wasn't long before I began to harbor a judgmental attitude toward them, toward my church, and toward church leadership for failing to protect me. My judgmental attitude took root, and I became bitter toward all people who claimed to hear God's voice. In my mind, they were flaky, odd, and low-key charlatans—this, coming from the person who was determined to spend the rest of her days understanding how and when God speaks to people.

By the time we were on our way to Kentucky, I wholly believed God spoke to the hearts of people, *but I had decided I wanted to find a church in Kentucky that believed He didn't*. Then, at least I could muffle these false prophecies and, more importantly, protect my young children from them. **I began exploring the possibility that the freedom and ability to hear God's voice was not worth the pain and confusion caused by people who misused it.**

I was squarely in the middle of proving my hypothesis (*by way of finding the church that did not believe God spoke to people outside the written word*) when God used the new pastor at the new church in Kentucky to speak to me.

God is hilarious.

So here we are. The contents of this lesson are the byproduct of God redirecting my heart and mind back to Scripture to understand how and why He uses other people to speak on His behalf—and just as importantly, how to know when to listen to, when to question, and when to run from a self-proclaimed prophet.

REFLECT AND ASSESS

Before we dive in, how comfortable are you with the possibility that God will speak to you through other people?

☐ **Not comfortable at all**
☒ **It depends on the person**
☐ **Very comfortable**

Can you think of a time when God spoke to you through someone else? How did you know it was God?

By more than one person
saying it, Counselling

Can you think of a time when a person claimed to be speaking on God's behalf, but it was most certainly not God? How did you know it was not God?

_____

_____

_____

_____

PROPHECY IN THE OLD TESTAMENT

In the Old Testament, God spoke through prophets regularly. Maybe you hear the word "prophet" and think of a person who sees the future—and that would be partially accurate. While the gift of prophecy certainly includes the ability to see the future, a prophet is far more than just a person with that ability. The Hebrew word for a prophet, _nabi, (naw-bee')_ comes from the term _niv sefatayim_ meaning "fruit of the lips." It literally means a spokesman or speaker.

So, a prophet is basically a spokesman for God, a person chosen by God to speak to people on God's behalf and convey a message or teaching. In addition, prophets in the Bible were role models of holiness, scholarship, and closeness to God. They set the standards for the entire community.[42]

Jeremiah offers a classic description of the relationship between the Lord and his prophet. Read the entire chapter below and answer the questions that follow.

Jeremiah 1

1 The words of Jeremiah son of Hilkiah, one of the priests at Anathoth in the territory of Benjamin. 2 The word of the Lord came to him in the thirteenth year of the reign of Josiah son of Amon king of Judah, 3 and through the reign of Jehoiakim son of Josiah king of Judah, down to the fifth month of the eleventh year of Zedekiah son of Josiah king of Judah, when the people of Jerusalem went into exile.

4 The word of the Lord came to me, saying,

5 "Before I formed you in the womb I knew you,
    before you were born I set you apart;
    I appointed you as a prophet to the nations."

6 "Alas, Sovereign Lord," I said, "I do not know how to speak; I am too young."

7 But the Lord said to me, "Do not say, 'I am too young.' You must go to everyone I send you to and say whatever I command you. **8** Do not be afraid of them, for I am with you and will rescue you," declares the Lord.

9 Then the Lord reached out his hand and touched my mouth and said to me, "I have put my words in your mouth. **10** See, today I appoint you over nations and kingdoms to uproot and tear down, to destroy and over-throw, to build and to plant."

11 The word of the Lord came to me: "What do you see, Jeremiah?"
"I see the branch of an almond tree," I replied.

12 The Lord said to me, "You have seen correctly, for I am watching to see that my word is fulfilled."

13 The word of the Lord came to me again: "What do you see?"

"I see a pot that is boiling," I answered. "It is tilting toward us from the north."

14 The Lord said to me, "From the north disaster will be poured out on all who live in the land. **15** I am about to summon all the peoples of the northern kingdoms," declares the Lord.

"Their kings will come and set up their thrones
    in the entrance of the gates of Jerusalem;
they will come against all her surrounding walls
    and against all the towns of Judah.

16 I will pronounce my judgments on my people
    because of their wickedness in forsaking me,

in burning incense to other gods
  and in worshiping what their hands have made.

17 *"Get yourself ready! Stand up and say to them whatever I command you. Do not be terrified by them, or I will terrify you before them. 18 Today I have made you a fortified city, an iron pillar and a bronze wall to stand against the whole land—against the kings of Judah, its officials, its priests and the people of the land. 19 They will fight against you but will not overcome you, for I am with you and will rescue you," declares the Lord.*

✿

1. The prophet of God was only allowed to speak the words God had given him—nothing more, and nothing less. Go back and underline or highlight all the verses suggesting this.

2. Sometimes God gave the prophet exact words, but sometimes God spoke to the prophets using other methods. What other method is demonstrated here? (vv. 11-13)

_____

3. The role of the prophet could be dangerous and scary, especially when the prophet had to deliver news the people did not like. What statements in this chapter indicate this?

_____

_____

_____

4. What promise did God make to Jeremiah to overcome his fear of the people? (v. 19)

_____

_____

_____

The Apostle Peter summarized the role of the Old Testament prophet beautifully in **2 Peter 1:21**. Find that verse in your Bible and write it word-for-word.

_____

_____

_____

_____

_____

Sometimes the only person **in an entire generation to hear God's voice** would be the prophet of God. Consequently, prophets were held to a very high standard.

In your Bible find **Deuteronomy 18:15-22** and answer the following questions.

1. What happened to the prophet who spoke in God's name, but did not speak what God commanded? (v. 20)

_____

2. What happened to the prophet of God who spoke in the name of other gods? (Also v. 20)

_____

3. How were the people to know whether or not the message was from the Lord? (v. 22)

_____

The testing of prophecies was common in that time. In some cultures, prophecies were tested to evaluate their validity by getting another opinion. Royal written records were kept about prophecies in order to check their fulfillment or nonfulfillment. In this way prophecies could be tested over a long period of time if necessary.[43]

Now turn to **Ezekiel 3:16-21**

1. In verses 18-20 God tells Ezekiel that if He tells the prophet to warn the people to turn from their sin, **but Ezekiel failed to warn** them, two things would happen. What were the two consequences?

_____

_____

2. What would happen if **the prophet warned the people as God commanded,** and the people obeyed and turned from their sin? (v. 21)

_____

_____

Finally, turn to **Ezekiel 13**. Read the entire chapter and summarize briefly in your own words how God felt about false prophecy. Be sure to note the impact false prophets had on God's people. What did God say He would do to the false prophets? What would God do to His people to whom the false prophets lied?

_____

_____

_____

_____

_____

_____

SUMMARY

- If a prophet of God misrepresented the word of God in any way, he would die.

- If a prophet of God spoke in the name of any other god, he would die.

- If a prophet of God failed to speak a warning (namely, that the people would die unless they turned from their sin) the people would still die in their sin, and the prophet would share in the punishment that would come on the people (i.e., they would all die).

- If a prophet led God's people astray, God would destroy the prophet, but set His people free and save them.

In short, the burden of proof rested on the shoulders of the prophet himself. He was responsible to hear God and speak exactly what he heard. If he led anyone astray, God punished him by death, and protected the recipients of the false prophecy.

PROPHECY IN THE NEW TESTAMENT

In the New Testament, God lives in the hearts of His people. That's you and me—the Church. He speaks to each of us intimately and directly. Yet, God still anoints some with a special gift of prophecy or calls them to the office of "prophet." According to **1 Corinthians 12**, the Church functions as a body where each person has a special function within it. The Spirit of God distributes gifts to each one of us and each gift is vital to the overall health and function of the Church. Prophecy is one of the many gifts of the Holy Spirit. (**1 Corinthians 12** may be familiar to you, but you may want to read it now to give yourself a refresher.)

In your Bible read **Romans 12:3-8**. What should you do if your gift is "prophecy"? (v. 6)

_____

In your Bible, look up **Ephesians 4:11-12**. What is the purpose of prophets according to this verse?

_____

_____

_____

Read the excerpt from **1 Corinthians 14** below and answer the questions that follow. (I've omitted portions of this chapter for brevity, but I encourage you to read the entire chapter in your Bible as additional reading.)

1 *Follow the way of love and eagerly desire gifts of the Spirit, especially prophecy.* **2** *For anyone who speaks in a tongue does not speak to people but to God. Indeed, no one understands them; they utter mysteries by the Spirit.* **3** *But the one who prophesies speaks to people for their strengthening, encouraging and comfort.* **4** *Anyone who speaks in a tongue edifies themselves, but the one who prophesies edifies the church.* **5** *I would like every one of you to speak in tongues, but I would rather have you prophesy. The one who prophesies is greater than the one who speaks in tongues, unless someone interprets, so that the church may be edified.*

6 *Now, brothers and sisters, if I come to you and speak in tongues, what good will I be to you, unless I bring you some revelation or knowledge or prophecy or word of instruction? ...*

9 *So it is with you. Unless you speak intelligible words with your tongue, how will anyone know what you are saying? You will just be speaking into the air...*

12 *So it is with you. Since you are eager for gifts of the Spirit, try to excel in those that build up the church....*

18 *I thank God that I speak in tongues more than all of you.* **19** *But in the church I would rather speak five intelligible words to instruct others than ten thousand words in a tongue....*

23 So if the whole church comes together and everyone speaks in tongues, and inquirers or unbelievers come in, will they not say that you are out of your mind? 24 But if an unbeliever or an inquirer comes in while everyone is prophesying, they are convicted of sin and are brought under judgment by all, 25 as the secrets of their hearts are laid bare. So they will fall down and worship God, exclaiming, "God is really among you!"

26 What then shall we say, brothers and sisters? When you come together, each of you has a hymn, or a word of instruction, a revelation, a tongue or an interpretation. Everything must be done so that the church may be built up....

29 Two or three prophets should speak, and the others should weigh carefully what is said. 30 And if a revelation comes to someone who is sitting down, the first speaker should stop. 31 For you can all prophesy in turn so that everyone may be instructed and encouraged. 32 The spirits of prophets are subject to the control of prophets. 33 For God is not a God of disorder but of peace—as in all the congregations of the Lord's people....

39 Therefore, my brothers and sisters, be eager to prophesy, and do not forbid speaking in tongues. 40 But everything should be done in a fitting and orderly way.

Clearly, in the New Testament, the role of prophet has been redefined. Since we now have access to the Holy Spirit directly, the prophet is no longer the sole spokesperson for God. Yet, prophets still have a very important role in the Church.

Complete the chart below by identifying the role and duties of the New Testament prophet according to the passages we just read:

Eph 4:11-12	To prepare God's people for works of _____
Eph 4:11-12, 1 Cor 14:12, 26	To _____ _____ the Body of Christ
1 Cor 14:3	To _____, encourage, and _____

1 Cor 14:4	To _____ the Church
1 Cor 14:19, 31	To _____ and encourage
1 Cor 14:24-25	To convict _____ of sin and reveal the secrets of their hearts, so they fall down and worship God.

Not only has the role of prophet shifted, but so has the "burden of proof." Now, the authenticity of the prophecy rests with **the hearer** as opposed to **the prophet!**

Look back at **1 Corinthians 14** and circle **verse 29**. When a prophet speaks in church, who should test what is said?

_____

In your Bible, find **1 Thessalonians 5:19-24**.

Write **1 Thessalonians 5:19-20** word-for-word:

_____

_____

_____

The NIV says, "Do not treat prophecies with contempt."

Other translations say
"Don't scoff at prophecies," NLT
"Don't despise prophecies," ESV
"Don't ignore prophecies," CEV
"Don't reject prophecies." Aramaic Bible in Plain English

Apparently, the early church had the same problem I had—namely, people walking around claiming to be speaking on God's behalf, but saying stupid, false, or dangerous things. As a result, the church not only became skeptical, but they actually started rejecting all prophecies. I totally understand how that happens. The Apostle Paul instructs us to *test everything and only hold onto what is good.*

But, what is a "good prophecy"? It must meet the same criteria of any other "voice" in question. In other words, in order to pass the "good" test, a prophecy must:

❀ align with God's written word and must make sense in light of God's motives and purposes of speaking, as we learned in Lesson Two.

In your Bibles read **Acts 17:10-12**.

Who was teaching the word of God?

_____

What did the Bereans do, exactly?

_____

_____

How are the Bereans described here?

_____

_____

❀ meet the criteria specifically for a prophecy as described in **Ephesians 4 and 1 Corinthians 14** (the chart you completed earlier in this lesson).

❀ bring God's peace, as mentioned in both **1 Thessalonians 5:23** and **1 Corinthians 14:33**. As we've already learned in Lesson Six, God's voice and God's peace are inseparable.

❋ align with what you already know to be true and be consistent with what God has already spoken to you. Or if it is new information to you, it will be confirmed by God to you in other ways.

🔊 **Pause and Listen:** Are any verses jumping out to you? Is God bringing to mind a word spoken to you and clarifying whether or not it was Him speaking? Is He bringing to mind a person He is using in your life to speak His word to you? What is God saying to you right now?

_____

_____

_____

_____

_____

_____

IDENTIFYING GOD-HEARING PEOPLE

The nudge from God for me to lead our church's women's ministry came out of nowhere. It started as a simple idea in my mind—_I should lead the women's ministry._ But within a few weeks' time, the gentle nudge became a full-on mental preoccupation. Every day, I envisioned myself standing before the women of my congregation, teaching and encouraging. I saw myself sitting across the table from individual women spurring them toward their passions. I wrote up a full plan for launching a woman-to-woman mentor program and actually started writing the training. I designed a freaking logo!

Two important facts about me concerning this nudge:

Fact one: In the nearly three decades I've been an adult female in the Church, I never "did" women's ministry. I'm not sure why, but I had a skewed impression that women's ministries were shallow, emotional, one-dimensional, and often involved events called "teas" or "luncheons."

Fact two: At this time, I was in the middle of writing my first book, had my hands full with my kids, and quite simply wasn't looking for more stuff to do—which has been the summation of my life in some form since giving birth to my first child in 1997.

So, when I finally spilled my ideas to Jon over date night dinner, he was skeptical. He witnessed first-hand my nonexistent history with church women's ministry programs, my propensity toward becoming easily overwhelmed, and the lack of space in my schedule to take on a new leadership role. He was wise to doubt. But, if my heart pounding out of my chest was any indication of how excited I was, he was equally wise to encourage me to seek God more on the matter.

I was so certain it was God speaking to me that I fully expected a call from one of our pastors inviting me into the position. When that didn't happen, Jon encouraged me to talk directly to our executive pastor on Sunday and inquire. I am embarrassed to admit that I was so disconnected from our women's ministry that I did not even realize the position had been vacant for over a year—and yet, here I was, presuming God was calling me (!) to lead it. If I were completely off base, my pastor would let me know.

So on that Sunday morning when I had planned to have the conversation with my pastor, my friend, Ayisha, walked into church. I was volunteering at the children's sign-in counter, and she was there to check her children into their classes. Ayisha is one of my favorite people for a number of reasons, not the least of which is her ability to make me laugh harder than just about anyone. But more importantly, she speaks life into everyone she encounters, with an uncanny ability to bring out the best in her friends. Also, she has an undeniable gift of prophecy.

She walked in with a facetious smile, and said, "I need to talk to you."

"Okaaaay."

Then she walked right up to that children's ministry check-in counter, pointed at my face, and said, "You're supposed to lead our women's ministry."

And I was like, "WHAT!???? How did you know this?" I covered my head and stepped back and started laughing hysterically while also breaking out into a sweat and turning three shades of red. I may have spun around and also crouched on the floor behind the counter. (Despite my certainty that God speaks and my expectancy for Him to speak to me, it still shocks and thrills me every time.)

My reaction caused her to start jumping up and down yelling, "It's true! It's true! I knew it!"

Our jumping and crouching and yelling was causing quite a scene in the children's wing, so I shushed her and pulled her behind the counter, and whispered, "Why are you saying this to me?"

She explained that earlier in the week she sensed God was telling her to call me and tell me—which didn't make any sense to her either, for all the reasons *it made no sense to ANYONE!* And when she told her husband (who also makes me laugh), he was like, "You can't call her and tell her that! She's busy! She'll think you're crazy! Do NOT call Sandy and tell her 'God said you should lead the women's ministry.'"

And so she didn't.

Until she saw me.

Then she had to!

So, that morning, I talked to our executive pastor, who then talked to the senior pastor, who then talked to the church elders, who then prayed. And two months later, during our Sunday morning worship service, they officially installed me as Women's Ministry Leader.

God undeniably spoke to my heart. But He miraculously confirmed it through my trusted friend, and then through the leaders of my church.

❁

When someone says, "God said..." we (the Church, spirit-filled believers, the body of Christ) must judge not only *what the person says*, but also *who the person is*.

Yes, that means we are actually instructed to judge other people.

In your Bible read **Hebrews 13:7-9**. What should we consider in our leaders who speak the word of God?

_____

_____

The Message renders verses 7-9 this way (bolding mine): "Appreciate your pastoral leaders who gave you the Word of God. **Take a good look at the way they live, and let their faithfulness instruct you, as well as their truthfulness.** There should be a consistency that runs through us all. For Jesus doesn't change—yesterday, today, tomorrow, he's always totally himself."

The writer of Hebrews is telling us to submit to the godly leaders God places over us (I believe this would apply to pastors, as well as any of those from which we choose to learn), but he is also warning us to consider the outcome of their lives (their fruit), to take a close look at how they live, and to imitate only those actions consistent with a life filled with faith in Jesus Christ.

Now turn to **Matthew 7:15-20**. How does Jesus tell us to recognize false prophets?

_____

When you are choosing people to speak into your life (and yes, you DO have a choice who speaks into your life!) or into the lives of your children, it is vital you examine their words, their actions, their relationships, and their ministry for alignment to the word of God:

- They should be people who consistently demonstrate the fruit of the Spirit (love, joy, peace, patience, kindness, goodness, faithfulness, gentleness, and self-control).

- They should be lovers of God's word. You won't even need to ask them if they are—the proof will be peppered throughout the good words they speak. Jesus told us that a good man brings good things out of the good stored up in him (**Matthew 12:34-35**).

- They should be humble and wise and always point you toward Jesus.

There is a time and a place to rightly judge someone, and this is it. If someone is claiming to hear God on your behalf, you have a God-given responsibility to investigate further. This is not to be confused with *being judgmental*. We don't have a right to determine a person's motives or decide a person's eternal fate. But we can and should examine the fruit of a person's life to decide if their prophecy is good or bad. The accountability for modern-day prophet rests with you and me.

SUMMARY

- God will often use other people to speak to you. (And, hey! That means He will also use YOU to speak to other people!)

- In the Old Testament, God often spoke directly to His people through the prophets.

- Because they did not have direct access to God's word and were not yet filled with God's Spirit, the consequences for misrepresenting God's words were severe (death), and the burden of proof to accurately speak God's word rested with the prophet.

- In the New Testament, God sometimes speaks directly to His people through other people.

❀ But now, because we have access to the written word of God and to the Spirit of God, the burden of proof is on us—the hearer.

❀ We have the responsibility to judge both the validity of the message spoken (Is it consistent with God's word? Is it consistent with what God has already spoken to us? Does it align with God's purpose for speaking? Does it bring peace?) and the character of the speaker (Does this person bear fruit consistent with being a follower of Christ?).

❀ God did not leave us on our own to figure all this out. He gave us His Word, His Spirit, and each other. He will use all three to speak to us and lead us.

TEN INSIGHTS ON HEARING GOD THROUGH OTHER PEOPLE

In **Exodus 18** we find a practical passage often used by church leaders to illustrate the importance and process of delegation. But I find it to be just as practical in our discussion on hearing God's voice through other people. As we conclude this lesson, let's examine this chapter more closely and extract some final insights. I suggest you read **Exodus 18** in your Bible all the way through before we begin.

❀

Exodus 18

Now Jethro, the priest of Midian and father-in-law of Moses, heard of everything God had done for Moses and for his people Israel, and how the Lord had brought Israel out of Egypt.

2 After Moses had sent away his wife Zipporah, his father-in-law Jethro received her 3 and her two sons. One son was named Gershom, for Moses said, "I have become a foreigner in a foreign land"; 4 and the other was named Eliezer, for he said, "My father's God was my helper; he saved me from the sword of Pharaoh."

5 Jethro, Moses' father-in-law, together with Moses' sons and wife, came to him in the wilderness, where he was camped near the mountain of God. 6 Jethro had sent word to him, "I, your father-in-law Jethro, am coming to you with your wife and her two sons."

Insight 1. God will orchestrate the scenarios for godly people to speak into your life.

Moses didn't call for Jethro and wasn't expecting Jethro, but Moses made himself available when Jethro showed up. This is all part of "inclining your ear to hear," as we discussed in Lesson Three. When we position ourselves to hear, God will work out the details of when and how.

7 So Moses went out to meet his father-in-law and bowed down and kissed him. They greeted each other and then went into the tent. 8 Moses told his father-in-law about everything the Lord had done to Pharaoh and the Egyptians for Israel's sake and about all the hardships they had met along the way and how the Lord had saved them.

9 Jethro was delighted to hear about all the good things the Lord had done for Israel in rescuing them from the hand of the Egyptians. 10 He said, "Praise be to the Lord, who rescued you from the hand of the Egyptians and of Pharaoh, and who rescued the people from the hand of the Egyptians. 11 Now I know that the Lord is greater than all other gods, for he did this to those who had treated Israel arrogantly." 12 Then Jethro, Moses' father-in-law, brought a burnt offering and other sacrifices to God, and Aaron came with all the elders of Israel to eat a meal with Moses' father-in-law in the presence of God.

Insight 2. God will use people who love God and love you to speak into your life.

Jethro was in for a family visit, during which he spent time listening to Moses talk about God and His deliverance of the Israelites, and also about Moses and his hardships in leading. People who take the time to find out where we are and what we need are prime candidates for speaking God's words to us. Even though Jethro was a Gentile, he still made a bold declaration of faith and worship to God. Here, we see him praising God, bringing burnt offerings to God, and spending time in God's presence. Jethro loved Moses and Moses clearly held Jethro in high esteem.

13 *The next day Moses took his seat to serve as judge for the people, and they stood around him from morning till evening.* **14** *When his father-in-law saw all that Moses was doing for the people, he said, "What is this you are doing for the people? Why do you alone sit as judge, while all these people stand around you from morning till evening?"*

Insight 3. Even when you are in the center of God's will, you could be missing something.

Moses was doing what he thought to be God's will and purpose for his life. Yet he was running himself into the ground, and didn't even recognize it. Isn't this often the case? We are doing everything we know to be right and can't figure out why we are so spent, tired, and worn out. I don't know about you, but I find it comforting that even Moses (the most humble man on the face of the earth and the one to whom God spoke clearly and most often) got stuck. And I find it even more comforting that God did not leave him there, but sent someone to show him the way out.

15 *Moses answered him, "Because the people come to me to seek God's will.* **16** *Whenever they have a dispute, it is brought to me, and I decide between the parties and inform them of God's decrees and instructions."* **17** *Moses' father-in-law replied, "What you are doing is not good."*

Insight 4. It's unwise to continually go to the same person, over and over, to hear God for you.

The people knew Moses was a man of God who heard God's voice clearly. How very tempting it would be to take every matter, big and small, to a guy like that. I've done that, too. We find that God-fearing, God-hearing person who seems so wise, so competent, so God-like and we suck the life out of them. Before we know it, we've stopped going to God all together.

❋

18 *You and these people who come to you will only wear yourselves out. The work is too heavy for you; you cannot handle it alone.*

Insight 5. A true God-fearing, God-hearing person will have a heart-felt concern for you, your physical and emotional well being, for your relationship with the Lord and for the good of the Church as a whole.

I've had many people who barely knew me try to speak into my life. In the age of social media, where complete strangers have access to details about our lives, this is becoming more common. Unless God confirms it to you through His peace, you are under no obligation to listen to people who are not concerned with you as a human.

❋

19 *Listen now to me and I will give you some advice, and may God be with you. You must be the people's representative before God and bring their disputes to him.* **20** *Teach them his decrees and instructions, and show them the way they are to live and how they are to behave.*

Insight 6. A God-fearing, God-hearing person will point you to God. This person will also be helpful in identifying and defining your purpose and role in the Body of Christ.

Two ways I can tell immediately if a person is sensitive to God's voice on my behalf:

❋   They point me to Jesus to "test" what they are telling me.

❋   They articulate recurring themes in my life that God has already spoken to me in other ways.

For example, God has used many people to encourage me in my writing—even people who never read a word I had written. God has also used many people to reinforce my primary roles as wife and mother, especially during times when I'm seeking direction or confirmation in those areas. Sometimes we, like Moses, may understand our gifts and talents, but may be at a loss for how to correctly apply them in our current season. Jethro told Moses he was right to be a judge but he was carrying out the specifics of his duties incorrectly.

❀

21 *But select capable men from all the people—men who fear God, trust-worthy men who hate dishonest gain—and appoint them as officials over thousands, hundreds, fifties and tens.* **22** *Have them serve as judges for the people at all times, but have them bring every difficult case to you; the simple cases they can decide themselves. That will make your load lighter, because they will share it with you.*

Insight 7. God places different people in our lives at various levels of authority to speak at different times and for different purposes.

Obviously, Jethro's instructions show the wisdom of delegation. But I think it is also a beautiful illustration of how God uses different people to serve different roles in our lives. Look around. God has certainly placed many capable men and women around you for specific purposes.

Maybe you have a best friend who is your "everyday voice." She's the one who is the sounding board to your rants, the one who encourages you to love your spouse and your kids, the one who encourages you to rest when you're spent, or pushes you to go on when you're discouraged. She is the one who tells you to pursue your dreams and goals and lets you bounce off your crazy ideas.

Maybe you also have a mentor you go to with financial questions or marriage questions. Maybe you know a woman a few steps ahead of you whom you call when you have a difficult parenting situation. You don't call her every day, but you know she's there to talk through a more complex issue whenever you need her.

Finally, you may also have a pastor, a ministry leader, or a therapist—a person you see about deeper questions of calling, purpose, or theology. This would be your "Moses."

When you are looking for people to speak into your life, you don't need one person who can be all and hear all for you. In fact, that's not God's way. God will bring multiple people to speak to you at different levels.

✽

23 *If you do this and God so commands, you will be able to stand the strain, and all these people will go home satisfied."*

Insight 8. Everyone benefits when we obey the voice of God.

Here's how The Message renders that verse:

If you handle the work this way, you'll have the strength to carry out whatever God commands you, and the people in their settings will flourish also.

Has it crossed your mind, *"What's the point?"* Since we started this study, have you wondered if it really matters if you hear God's voice at all? Well, here's your answer: When you listen to and obey God's voice, you will have the strength to carry out God's will for your life and **all the people you impact will flourish also**. It's not only about you. It's about your kids and your neighbors and your coworkers and all the people God has placed in your life. It's about the Church and the kingdom of God. Everyone benefits from you listening to and obeying God's voice.

✽

24 *Moses listened to his father-in-law and did everything he said.* **25** *He chose capable men from all Israel and made them leaders of the people, officials over thousands, hundreds, fifties and tens.* **26** *They served as judges for the people at all times. The difficult cases they brought to Moses, but the simple ones they decided themselves.*

Insight 9. If God uses someone to speak into your life, obey.

As we learned in Lesson Five, obedience is a key to future hearing. If you are having a difficult time hearing God, I would suggest you go back to the very last thing you know for certain He said, and start there.

For years, God nudged me to get up in the morning for prayer—before school as a college student, then before work as a young career woman, and then before kids as a new mom (like I said, YEARS!). It was hard for me. I was not a morning person. I tried and failed more times than I can count. But, often when I'd become desperate to hear God, I'd pray and inquire why He wasn't speaking to me. The answer I'd get would be, "I told you to get up early and seek Me. You haven't done that yet." When I finally disciplined myself to do it, the flood-gates opened, and I began hearing God with such clarity, it shocked me. For you, it may not be getting up early to pray. But whatever it is God speaks to you, obey it.

27 *Then Moses sent his father-in-law on his way, and Jethro returned to his own country.*

Insight 10. A real God-fearing, God-hearing person will know when to say goodbye.

God places people in our lives to play certain roles for specific seasons. Look for the ones He has planted all around you. They are there. And when it's time for them or for you to move on, it's okay! God won't ever leave you. And when you need other people to speak God's word to you, He will be certain to guide them onto your path.

> A
> P
> P
> L
> Y
>
> Think through the people in your life. Who is your "everyday" person? Who can you take more difficult matters to? Who is your "Moses"? Write their names here. If you cannot think of anyone in your life to fill one or more of these roles, pray and ask God to provide this person for you.
>
> *My everyday person is my sister Debbie.*
> *My Moses was my dear friend Jim,*
> *He passed away, now its Marie. Also*
> *I have a friend Chris who is a helper.*

FOR DISCUSSION

Has God ever used you to speak to someone? How did you know it was God? How did the recipient respond?

_____

_____

_____

_____

_____

_____

_____

_____

_____

_____

_____

_____

_____

_____

_____

_____

_____

_____

❀ God uses people to speak to us in many ways other than direct person-to-person conversations. Consider how God has used people through books, music, social media, etc., to speak to you. Share a few examples with your group.

_____

_____

_____

_____

_____

_____

_____

_____

_____

_____

_____

_____

_____

_____

_____

_____

_____

_____

❋ What might be an appropriate Biblical response to someone who prophesies to you, but is not speaking the truth of God? Would you address the error or would you simply ignore the prophecy?

_____

_____

_____

_____

_____

_____

_____

_____

_____

_____

_____

_____

_____

_____

_____

_____

_____

_____

_____

❁ Matthew 7 begins, "Do not judge or you too will be judged." This is a passage that is often quoted to mean, "You have no right to judge me." Read that passage in context, (Matthew 7:1-5) and consider what you learned in this lesson about judging someone's fruit. Discuss what you think Jesus was saying. Do you believe the passage saying that we never have the right or duty to judge someone? Why or why not?

_____

_____

_____

_____

_____

_____

_____

_____

_____

_____

_____

_____

_____

_____

_____

_____

❀ What is your biggest takeaway from this lesson?

_____

_____

_____

_____

_____

_____

_____

_____

_____

_____

_____

_____

_____

_____

_____

_____

_____

Conclusion

When God is Silent

"O God, do not remain silent, do not turn a deaf ear, do not stand aloof, O God."

PSALM 83:1

I was in the shower at 4 am. After nine long months of waiting, I was about to give birth to my daughter, Rebekah. Because of prior health complications, she would enter our lives by way of scheduled cesarean section. Jon and I took one last "pregnancy picture" of me and my giant belly standing in front of the fireplace, picked up the bags I had packed weeks prior, and headed to the hospital. We arrived while it was still dark, and spent most of the morning waiting—waiting for a room, waiting for the nurse to insert the IV (several failed attempts), waiting for *another* nurse who could actually find the vein in my arm(!), waiting for my doctor to arrive...

Now, after six hours of waiting (and multiple puncture holes on my forearm), I was strapped to a table, flat on my back, waiting again for the procedure to begin.

I was completely numb from the chest down with a curtain hanging between me and the surgeons, blocking my view entirely. Jon stood at my side holding my hand, with a bird's-eye view of both my face and my belly. I waited patiently (okay, not patiently!) again. Jon and I exchanged nervous smiles.

The pregnancy had been of the "long and difficult" variety. We had buried our nine-month-old son, Noah, a few weeks before discovering I was pregnant with Rebekah, making this pregnancy complex from the outset. Then, five months into the pregnancy, we received the long-awaited results of Noah's autopsy revealing two rare medical conditions that would potentially affect my current pregnancy and fatally harm my new baby.[44] This news catapulted me into a high-risk category and required me to visit a maternal fetal specialist several times a week to monitor Rebekah's growth in utero. Keeping Rebekah alive became my full-time job. Which, oddly, was a welcome distraction from my other full-time job: grieving the loss of my son.

So, even though I was in the final stretch of this long road, I was done. If I had feeling in my legs, I would have been tapping my foot. If my arms were not strapped to the table, I would have been wringing my hands. All I wanted was for the doctor to get my baby girl out alive and hand her to me so I could go home and live my life.

Because of my rare health conditions, my doctor had invited a team of medical students and interns to observe the procedure. There must have been 10 of them hovering quietly over my lower half for the better part of an hour. I could only see the tops of their heads, but their ominous presence was unnerving. None of them said a word. Not to me, not to Jon. Ugh.

I looked at Jon and smiled again and took another deep breath...*waiting.*

Did I mention I was done?

Jon was quiet, too. He's normally quiet, so this was no big deal. I mean, I would have appreciated some sort of update, but I knew he'd give me a play-by-play once the doctors began to cut. And yet, lying on that table immobile, my mind raced with questions.

When are they going to get started?

What in the world is taking so long?

What are they doing down there anyway?

Why haven't they begun the surgery?

Why is no one telling me anything?

How hard is it to cut me open and pull out a baby?

Because, so help me God, if someone does not say something soon, I'm gonna grab a scalpel and do it myself. (Not technically a question.)

Finally, I whispered to my husband, "I wish they would hurry up and get started—can you please ask them when they are going to start the C-section?"

Jon turned to me, leaned down, and in his calmest voice said, "Honey, your guts are all over the table."

"Ahhh! WHAT? They are?!"

I was shocked. I had no idea. I felt nothing—neither a tug nor a twitch. **And because no one was talking to me, I assumed nothing was happening.** Moments later my doctor held up my beautiful baby girl, and just like that, my life changed forever by Rebekah's entrance into the world.

❋

When we can't hear God's voice, it's tempting to assume nothing is happening.

I know some of you are in a season of waiting right now. Waiting for circumstances to change. Waiting for someone to act. Waiting for healing. Waiting for a new opportunity. Waiting for an open door. Waiting for joy. Waiting for peace. Waiting to hear something—*anything*—from Heaven. You know something is supposed to be happening, but you can't see it, you can't feel it, and no one's talking.

This is precisely why some of you picked up this Bible study and why you diligently worked through it all the way to the end: **You are waiting for God to say something to you.**

We established at the beginning and learned all throughout these lessons that God speaks to His people, absolutely and undeniably. The first act we see in Scripture is God speaking, and we see Him continuing to speak until the very last sentence of the last book. I've shared with you some of the most notable examples of God speaking in Scripture and examples of Him speaking directly to me. I hope as we conclude our time together, you at least understand this: **God speaks to His people!** If we are not experiencing this beautiful and life-giving truth of Scripture in our own lives, then we should figure out why.

To be clear, if you are still confused about God's voice or can't hear God on the regular, you should not automatically assume you've done something wrong. You will have times—even after completing this study— when you aren't sure if the voice in your head is God or just you. And you will have times when you don't hear a thing. Then you'll have times when you *think* you hear Him, but you'll need to ask Him for confirmation and seek and pray and fast and rebuke the Devil and starve the flesh before you'll know for sure.

This is normal. *You are normal.*

It doesn't mean you are immature or ungodly or doing anything wrong. It means you are a small human with limited understanding dealing with the Almighty and Limitless God. It means you are still learning how to discern His voice over all the others, and that's okay. This is a life-long pursuit.

> *"Being uncertain doesn't mean you haven't heard.*
> *Remember too that scientists check their results by rerunning*
> *experiments. We should be so humble."*
> **Dallas Willard**[45]

So, take heart. All of us will have times we can't identify the voice we are hearing. All of us will have times we can't hear God at all. As we learned throughout this study, God has revealed to us how to posture ourselves to be "good listeners."

Sometimes God is speaking but we are not listening.

If you are continually having trouble hearing Him—if you have gotten to the end of this study and you still feel lost and confused about God's voice—I'd suggest you start with what you've learned about inclining your ear to hear. Humble yourself before God and ask yourself these questions based on **The 5 Keys to Becoming a Good Listener**:

❀   Am I seeking a relationship with God? Or am I merely seeking His voice, His direction, or His provision?

❀   Am I immersing myself in God's word? Do I spend time daily reading, studying, and meditating on Scripture, so God can speak to me through His word and help me understand God's language? Or am I allowing days or weeks to go by before I pick up my Bible?

❀ Am I making room in my life for God to speak to me? Am I carving out periods of time every day where I am silent before Him? Or am I constantly filling my mind with information and my days with activity?

❀ Am I approaching God with a posture of humility? Do I rely on Him solely for everything I need? Do I trust Him with my life and my future? Am I willing to accept whatever He says, even if it's not what I want to hear? Or have I demanded God to speak to me on my terms?

❀ Am I walking in obedience to what I know to be true? Or has God already told me what to do, but I have failed to obey?

If you approach God in this way, He will lovingly reveal to you where you need to pivot or focus your attention. He is your Father and He wants you to know and hear Him more than you want to know and hear Him! He will not leave you in the dark. If you walk away from this study with any kernel of truth, please let it be this.

A few years ago, I received a text from a parent of one of my child's friends. She shared with me a few screen shots of an inappropriate text exchange between her child and mine. (#ittakesavillage) I thanked her and went up to my child's room to address the issue. But rather than marching up with all guns blazing, I knocked on the door, opened it quietly and calmly, walked in, and sat down on the floor opposite my child.

I didn't say a word.

I just looked the child in the eye and blinked.

And waited.

Silently.

Child: *What?*

Me: *silence*

Child: *What?!?*

Me: *blink* *blink*

Child: *Mom, you're freaking me out. What do you want?*

Me: *Do you have something to confess to me?*

Child: *What are you talking about? *Nervous shifting**

Me: *silence*

Then the most amazing thing happened. The child not only confessed the transgression at hand, but also confessed every questionable action taken in the previous month. (I had to use my best poker face as the words started pouring out of the child's mouth.) I know that process was uncomfortable for my child. But not nearly as uncomfortable as bearing the weight of hidden sin. We were able to deal with all the issues at once, administer the appropriate consequences, and continue with our lives.

Sometimes God uses strategic silence to reveal the sin in your heart.

The Bible says that God left Hezekiah to *"test him and to know everything that was in his heart."* (**2 Chronicles 32:31**). God already knows what's in our hearts. He's not waiting for us to reveal it *to Him*. He's waiting for us to reveal it *to ourselves.* The truth is, we don't always know what's in our hearts until God is sitting silently across the metaphorical room, blinking, waiting.

Sin always clogs communication between you and God. **Psalm 66:18** says, *"If I had cherished sin in my heart, the Lord would not have listened..."* If you can't hear the voice of God, examine your heart for sin. The condition of your heart is of utmost importance to God and should be equally important to you. Everything you do flows from it. (**Proverbs 4:23**) When your heart is diseased with sin, God's voice is muted. So, as you approach God, ask Him to reveal to you any of the following potential heart conditions:

An unforgiving heart

Matthew 6:14-15 says, *"For if you forgive men when they sin against you, your heavenly Father will also forgive you. But if you do not forgive men their sins,* **your Father will not forgive your sins.***"*

Jesus spoke this truth in the context of The Lord's Prayer—when He was explaining to the disciples how to talk with God. Withholding forgiveness hinders communication between you and God.

Jesus reveals another facet of this concept in **Matthew 5:23-24** when He says *"Therefore, if you are offering your gift at the altar and there remember that your brother or sister has something against you, leave your gift there in front of the altar.* **First go and be reconciled to them;** *then come and offer your gift."*

If you can't hear God, first go and forgive those who have hurt you, offended you, or mistreated you, and then come back and try again. How we treat others, even in our hearts, has a direct effect on how well we hear God. Speaking of how we treat others...

An inconsiderate or disrespectful heart

I Peter 3:7 says, *"Husbands, in the same way be considerate as you live with your wives, and treat them with respect as the weaker partner and as heirs with you of the gracious gift of life,* **so that nothing will hinder your prayers.***"*

I confess...this is a biggie for me. When Heaven becomes silent, one of the first places I examine is how I've been treating Jon. I know technically it says "husbands," but a bad heart is a bad heart, no matter what the gender. When I'm irritable, impatient, and disrespectful to him, I can't hear God speak to me until I confess that sin and ask for forgiveness. In fact, I had to do this very thing this morning before I sat down to write this chapter. I'm still growing in this area, too.

A quarrelsome or covetous heart

James 4:1-3 says, *"What causes fights and quarrels among you? Don't they come from your desires that battle within you? You want something but don't get it. You kill and covet, but you cannot have what you want.*

You quarrel and fight. You do not have, because you do not ask God. When you ask, you do not receive, because you ask with wrong motives, that you may spend what you get on your pleasures."

Oh my goodness, another passage about how we treat others! Did you ever realize your ability to hear from God is so closely affiliated with how you treat people? When you fight and quarrel it affects God's response to you.

As a new Christian, I did not get this memo. My desire to win the world over to Jesus eclipsed my sense to be kind to them. In all my 18-year-old-new-convert-zeal, I'd engage in animated and angry theological debates with my friends, and then wonder why I couldn't hear God speak to me when I prayed. I'm sure my shouting was an effective evangelism strategy, leading multitudes of college students to the heart of Jesus. *Sigh* (P.S. If I tried to "witness" to you between the years of 1986 and 1991, I'm sorry for yelling.)

And, of course, this passage talks about motives, as well. If we find ourselves asking God for good things, *truly good things* (the job promotion, the pay increase, the relationship, the house, the car, the opportunity...) only to hear absolutely nothing from Heaven, we should ask God to reveal the true motives behind the request.

You guys. This is hard stuff. I'm not saying any of this is easy or fun. Self-examination is challenging, especially when we are trying to discern our own motives or flesh out deeply embedded sin. But taking advantage of the opportunity to confess and repent affords us the freedom to move forward with unencumbered communication and fellowship with God. It's hard, but it's good.

Sometimes we can't hear God because He's not speaking.

Sometimes the reason we can't hear God has nothing to do with our posture or our sin or our heart. He's not waiting for us to confess or repent or treat people well. That's right. Sometimes God is *actually-for-real*, silent.

Of course, you will always have access to Scripture, and God will always speak to you through that—so, technically, He won't be completely silent. But if you are looking for specific direction or revelation about your life, your circumstances, or your future outside of what God has already given you in Scripture, God may not speak this to you. Let's take a look at a few reasons why.

God is silent because He wants to protect you or protect someone else.

As a parent, I withhold information from my children all the time. When they were small, I'd sneak spinach into their smoothies. I'd intercept candy from Grandma so I could dole it out over time before they'd shoved it all in their mouths and vomit. I'd secretly sort through their toys and donate items they didn't play with. (And then when they'd say, "Where is my such-and-such toy?" I'd say, "I don't know." Because, technically, I didn't.)

As they got older, I'd meet privately with teachers to discuss school issues. I'd monitor text messages and Internet activity without their knowledge. I'd protect one child's dignity when the other children demanded to know why their sibling was grounded for a month.

At every stage of parenting, I have withheld intel from my kids because it was best for them, it was best for someone else, or they were too immature to handle it. I am always acting in love on their behalf, but I am not always forthright with every detail of every action I make.

This doesn't mean I'm not acting. It just means I'm not talking.

If you feel like you are strapped to a table and you can't see what's going on and no one is talking, understand that the silence does not necessarily indicate a lack of action on God's part, but rather a lack of perspective on yours. If you were granted a bird's-eye view of your life, you'd see the Great Physician on the other side of the curtain cutting away your fleshly desires, removing impurities that hinder your ability to love, and stitching wounds so deep you didn't even know you were hurt. But also, in His infinite love and mercy, you'd see Him protecting you from both the pain and the details of the procedure—namely, that your guts are all over the table. The curtain and the silence have a purpose—protecting you from information you would not be able to tolerate. When or if it's time for you to know, He will tell you.

God is silent because He wants you to choose.

One of the simultaneously thrilling and scary parts of parenting is seeing what our children do when they are not in our presence. When they go to school, are they kind? When they spend the night with a friend, are they respectful? When they go to Grandma's, do they say "please" and "thank you" and "excuse me"?

When they are alone in their college dorms and we no longer filter their Internet or stock their fridge or impose a curfew, will they choose wholesome content, nutritious food, and sleep?

When they get married and have babies and build homes, will they love sacrificially and provide diligently and give generously?

Dallas Willard said, "What a child does when not told what to do is the final indicator of what and who that child is."[46]

Independence is a privilege of maturity. When we are immature in our faith, God delights to lead us in big and small decisions. Some of my best memories of my early days of walking with God are of Him blowing my mind, showing up everywhere, and speaking through everything.

But as we mature, He delights just as much to watch us make decisions that demonstrate that our hearts and minds have been transformed into His image. As we mature in our faith, God awards us more freedom to choose because our identity is rooted in Him and our hearts beat in tandem with His. Like a loving parent, He is thrilled to watch us choose the humble, sacrificial path without being overtly and specifically told to do so.

And sometimes, I gotta believe that, at the end of the day, some choices will be equally honoring to Him—He simply wants us to make a decision and enjoy the journey.

God is silent so you will seek Him more.

Jesus invites us into a relationship where we approach Him and pursue Him. This is not a business transaction or a mathematical equation. This is not a cold, impersonal situation where we complete the online request form and receive a digital download of instructions. We can't plug in our destination and expect turn-by-turn navigation—He's not Google Maps. If He revealed to us the entire plan for our lives and explained every detail to us ahead of time, we'd have no incentive to know Him or follow Him.

Jesus said in **Matthew 7:7-11**, "*Ask and it will be given to you; seek and you will find; knock and the door will be opened to you. For everyone who asks receives; the one who seeks finds; and to the one who knocks, the door will be opened. Which of you, if your son asks for bread, will give him a stone? Or if he asks for a fish, will give him a snake? If you, then, though you are evil, know how to give good gifts to your children, how much more will your Father in heaven give good gifts to those who ask him!*"

He wants us to discover Him. He wants us to hunger and thirst for Him. His silence is sometimes just an invitation to go deeper and longer and harder in our search.

When I first started studying how to hear God's voice, I would say things like, "Why is God so cryptic? Why doesn't He just say it plainly? This will be one of my first questions I ask Him when I get to Heaven!"

I'll just say now: *I'm so thankful He doesn't just say it plainly!*

Now when God is silent or cryptic or whatever, I get a little excited, knowing He's inviting me into an adventure with Him. I can almost see a twinkle in His eye as He extends His hand to me. These adventures have become the biggest surprise and greatest delight of my walk with the Lord. The asking and the seeking and the knocking…and the digging and the sobbing and trying and the failing…it's all been worth it. And the best part is, He has so much more to show me and so much more to say.

I hope as you complete this study that you feel hopeful and encouraged, even if you can't hear Him as clearly or as often as you want to. This isn't the end of a Bible study but the beginning of an adventure with God. Have a blast.

Epilogue

My favorite books are the ones that end with all the loose ends securely tied and the story loops sufficiently closed. A task nearly impossible to accomplish in a work of non-fiction (this is real-life, people!), much less, a Bible study.

My story of learning to discern the voice of God began in the back of a church when God was leading us from our hometown of Toledo, Ohio to relocate to Jacksonville, Florida.

I shared with you in this book how we fell in love with that city—the people, the weather, the ocean—all of it. I also shared how I left Jacksonville kicking and screaming (quite literally). In eight short years it became home to me and our growing family. I didn't want to move.

But God, in His mercy toward me, spoke profoundly and sweetly through a pastor and a Psalm in the back of another church in Louisville, Kentucky. There, He confirmed to me that He would not let our feet slip, He would protect us from harm, and He would watch over our coming into that city and our going out of that city should that day ever come.

So, we dug in. We planted roots. We raised our kids. We attended the Kentucky Derby and built a house next to a horse farm! We were all in. For 16 years we did our best to love and serve the people of Louisville. Yet, even with all the effort to make Louisville our home, I always sensed that we'd eventually leave.

The timing of the writing of this book was indeed providential. I had tried multiple times to write this manuscript in different versions over the last 10 years, first through my blog and then through developing the material for classes I taught at church. During that time, I also wrote two different book proposals and shopped them to literary agents and publishers. The response to those attempts was a resounding, "We like you. We like your writing. But, we're not interested in a

Bible study. Sorry."

I was frustrated but not confused. While I know many people who need and desire the material in this book, I don't see Bible studies competing for the top spots on the best-sellers lists. Publishing is a business, after all. I get it.

And yet, I couldn't escape the sense that I needed to compile everything I have studied and learned and put it into one resource. It needed to be a book! And I simply couldn't wait for a literary agent or publisher to pick me. I had to obey the leading of the Holy Spirit and write.

So, in September 2019, I embarked on a one-year social media hiatus and completely cleared my writing and speaking calendar for the sole purpose of completing this manuscript to release September 2020.

Of course, I had no idea this would be the year of COVID-19—none of us did. While I fully acknowledge the severity of the coronavirus (my husband works in a hospital, so I get it, I promise) and the devastation it continues to cause physically and economically for the entire world, "quarantine" happens to be the perfect environment for book writing. I mean, everything is cancelled and we must stay home? Indefinitely?

Um. Okay.

I'm just saying, in the 10+ years I have tried to write and publish this material, I could not have chosen a better year to hunker down and get 'er done.

Even more unbelievable was that, while I was about halfway through writing this manuscript, a job offer practically fell onto my husband's lap. Literally, as I was working on the very lesson where I tell you how much I hated to leave Jacksonville, my husband was undergoing Zoom interviews in our basement (#COVID-19) for a new position that would move us back.

As I write this Epilogue, I'm sitting on my bed in an apartment in Jacksonville, Florida, surrounded by partially unpacked boxes. We arrived three weeks ago. I can hardly believe I'm here.

God's timing had me fully immersed in the study of hearing His voice at a time when I would need it the most. Even today, as I sit in temporary housing, waiting for our house to sell in Kentucky so we can buy a new house in Florida, I'm applying everything I've learned about hearing God speak to guide us in the final details of our relocation.

Indeed, my favorite stories are the ones that come full circle, where the main characters get closure and everyone lives happily ever after.

I don't know about the *happily ever after* part...again, this is real life. But I do think it's pretty cool of God, the Author of *this* story, to orchestrate the writing of this epilogue to be the exact time we would be coming back to where it all began.

Endnotes

Introduction

1. Willard, Dallas. (1884, 1993, 1999, 2012). *Hearing God: Developing a Conversational Relationship with God.* Downers Grove, IL: InterVarsity Press, 220.

2. Blackaby, Henry T. and Richard. (2002). *Hearing God's Voice.* Nashville, TN: Broadman and Holman Publishers, 48.

Lesson One

3. Why am I asking you to identify the audience? When doing a verse-by-verse study of Scripture, I'll sometimes ask you to identify certain markers. The specific details may seem irrelevant to the topic, but they are helpful in terms of understanding the context of the passage. In this case, it helps to know that Jesus was talking to both Pharisees and a general Jewish audience because they had such mixed reactions to His words.

4. NIV Study Bible Notes on Psalm 23:4, via Biblegateway.com.
https://www.biblegateway.com/passage/?search=Psalm+23:4&version=NIV

5. Insights for this lesson—specifically about sheep herding in the ancient Near East— were compiled and curated from the following sources: NIV Cultural Backgrounds Study Bible, Copyright © 2016 by Zondervan. Zondervan Illustrated Bible Backgrounds Commentary of the New Testament, Copyright © 2002. Expositor's Bible Commentary (Abridged Edition): New Testament, Copyright 2004. http://acharlie.tripod.com/shepherd.html

Lesson Two

6. Blackaby, Henry and Richard (2002). *Hearing God's Voice.* Nashville, TN: Broadman and Holman Publishers. 144.

7. Blackaby, 42

8. Eldredge, John. (2008). *Walking With God: Talk to Him. Hear From Him. Really.* Nashville, TN: Thomas Nelson. 13-14.

Lesson Three

9. www.goodreads.com/author/quotes/20333.Phillip_C_McGraw

10. Rydelnik, Michael and VanLaningham, Michael. (2014) *The Moody Bible Commentary.* Chicago, IL: Moody Publishers, 1581.

11. Moody Commentary, 1475 and NIV Cultural Backgrounds Study Bible, (2016), Zondervan via Biblegateway.com

12. Evans, Dr. Tony, (2017, Reprint 2018) *Discerning the Voice of God: How to Recognize when God Speaks.* Nashville, TN: Lifeway Press, 131.

13. These are the 73 Psalms that are attributed to David:

Psalms 3–9	Psalm 101	Psalm 131
Psalms 11–41	Psalm 103	Psalm 133
Psalms 51–65	Psalms 108–110	Psalms 138–145
Psalms 68–70	Psalm 122	
Psalm 86	Psalm 124	

14. Shirer, Priscilla, (2017, Reprint 2018) *Discerning the Voice of God: How to Recognize when God Speaks.* Nashville, TN: Lifeway Press, 86.

15. Blackaby, Henry T. and Richard. (2002). *Hearing God's Voice.* Nashville, TN: Broadman and Holman Publishers, 108.

16. Willard, Dallas. (1884, 1993, 1999, 2012). *Hearing God: Developing a Conversational Relationship with God.* Downers Grove, IL: InterVarsity Press, 212.

17. The Brant and Sherri Oddcast, Episode 1063, January 20, 2020.

Lesson Four

18. https://www.lifehack.org/377243/science-says-silence-much-more-important-our-brains-than-thought.

19. https://www.vox.com/recode/2020/1/6/21048116/tech-companies-time-well-spent-mobile-phone-usage-data.

20. https://www.telegraph.co.uk/news/uknews/2675430/The-average-person-only-gets-63-minutes-of-peace-and-quiet-a-day.html.

21. Buchanan, Mark, (2006) *The Rest of God: Restoring Your Soul By Restoring Sabbath.* Nashville, TN; W Publishing Group, a Division of Thomas Nelson. Inc., 178.

22. Foster, Richard J., (1998) *The Celebration of Discipline: The Path To Spiritual Growth.* New York, NY: Harper Collins, 97.

23. Buchanan, 196

24. For more on hurry and other practical ways to combat it, read my book *Finding Your Balance.*

25. Just kidding. I have never once, in my whole life, used the words thermonuclear engineering in a sentence or argued about it with a know-it-all. Is thermonuclear engineering a real thing? It sounds like a real thing. I don't even know.

26. Warren, Rick, (2002) *The Purpose-Driven Life: What on Earth am I Here For?* Grand Rapids, MI: Zondervan, Day 19.

27. Lewis, C.S. (2009) Mere Christianity, Revised and Enlarged Edition. New York, NY: Harper Collins, Book 3.

28. Murray, Andrew, (2004) *Humility, Updated Edition.* New Kensington, PA: Whitaker House, 94.

Lesson Five

29. Shirer, Priscilla (2017, Reprint 2018) *Discerning the Voice of God: How to Recognize When God Speaks, Revised and Expanded,* Nashville, TN: Lifeway Press, 34.

30. Blackaby, Henry T. and Richard. (2002). *Hearing God's Voice.* Nashville, TN: Broadman and Holman Publishers, 214

Lesson Six

31. Some would argue that we have a third part of our being called "the spirit." For our purposes, and for simplicity, I'm only distinguishing between our body and our soul. For an interesting discussion about whether we are a one-part, two-part, or three-part being, see Wayne Grudem's discussion here: https://zondervanacademic.com/blog/what-is-the-soul

32. I want to credit Priscilla Shirer for being the first to introduce me to this concept through her Bible study on discerning the voice of God. Prior to this, I wrongly assumed a person's conscience and God's voice were the same. If you want to learn more, see Priscilla Shirer's *Discerning the Voice of God: How to Recognize When God Speaks, Revised and Expanded*, 47-53.

33. I am not telling you to become a doormat and endure abuse. Please don't. If you are in a difficult marriage, please seek professional counseling. If you are in an abusive situation (verbal, emotional, or physical) please leave and find a safe place to stay, and then seek professional counseling.

34. This is a term coined and used by Ann Lamott.

Lesson Seven

35. https://www.dfa.cornell.edu/sites/default/files/detect-counterfeit.pdf

36. Brand, Chad Owen—General Editor (2015) *Holman Illustrated Bible Dictionary.* Nashville, TN: B&H Publishing Group, 577-578.

37. https://www.biblegateway.com/resources/dictionary-of-bible-themes/6166-flesh-sinful-nature

38. Brand, p. 369

39. Derby Day in Louisville is the biggest event of the year. The whole city goes nuts for a solid month. To ask when Derby Day is would be akin to asking when New Year's Day is—only more outrageous. Like, what planet are you from? It's the first Saturday of May, by the way. Except for the year I'm writing this book, 2020. This year, because of COVID-19, the Kentucky Derby has been rescheduled for Saturday, September 5. This is the first time since 1945 that the Derby has been postponed.

40. https://www.vox.com/identities/2017/11/10/16630178/study-spiritual-but-not-religious; https://www.barna.com/research/meet-spiritual-not-religious/

41. For a fantastic study on this passage, I highly recommend you dig deeper with Priscilla Shirer's study, *The Armor of God*.

Lesson Eight

42. http://www.jewfaq.org/prophet.htm where there is also a comprehensive list of all the prophets in the Old Testament.

43. NIV Cultural Backgrounds Study Bible via Biblegateway.com

Conclusion

44. The two rare medical conditions are called Maternal Floor Infarction and LCHAD. Maternal Floor Infarction affected me during my pregnancy. It is characterized by deposition of fibrinoid material in the maternal surface and intervillous spaces of the placenta. The cause remains uncertain; however, it has clearly been associated with significant perinatal morbidity and mortality including stillbirths, recurrent pregnancy loss, premature delivery, and intrauterine growth restriction. While this is an extremely rare condition, the chances of it occurring in subsequent pregnancies are very high. Long-chain 3-hydroxyacyl-CoA dehydrogenase or LCHAD affected Noah directly. It is a

rare condition that prevents the body from converting certain fats to energy, particularly during periods of fasting—like when a baby starts to sleep through the night or when a child has reflux. Signs and symptoms of LCHAD deficiency typically appear during infancy or early childhood and can include feeding difficulties, lack of energy (lethargy), low blood sugar (hypoglycemia), weak muscle tone (hypotonia), liver problems, and abnormalities in the light-sensitive tissue at the back of the eye. Later in childhood, people with this condition may experience muscle pain, breakdown of muscle tissue, and a loss of sensation in their arms and legs (peripheral neuropathy). Individuals with LCHAD deficiency are also at risk for serious heart problems, breathing difficulties, coma, and sudden death. Problems related to LCHAD deficiency can be triggered when the body is under stress, for example during periods of fasting, illnesses such as viral infections, or weather extremes. The incidence of LCHAD deficiency is unknown. One estimate, based on a Finnish population, indicates that 1 in 62,000 pregnancies is affected by this disorder. In the United States, the incidence is probably much lower. My doctor told me that the chances of me having both MFI and LCHAD in the same pregnancy were about 1 in 1,000,000. We do know that LCHAD is passed down by a recessive gene mutation that must be possessed by each parent. In other words, Jon and I both carry the recessive gene for LCHAD and the disease affects neither of us. This means our biological children have a 25% chance of being affected, a 50% chance of being unaffected carriers of the mutation (like Jon and me), and a 25% chance of not carrying the gene at all. Rebekah does not carry the gene for LCHAD, thank God. This disorder is treatable if you know your child has it, but we did not know about Noah's diagnosis until we received the results of his autopsy. Many states now screen newborns for LCHAD as part of their routine infant screenings at birth. To determine if your state screens for LCHAD at birth, see https://www.babysfirsttest.org/newborn-screening/states.

45. Willard, Dallas. (1884, 1993, 1999, 2012). *Hearing God: Developing a Conversational Relationship with God.* Downers Grove, IL: InterVarsity Press, 261.

46. Ibid., 220.

Acknowledgments

Since I've been writing this book in some form for well over two decades, I am one hundred percent positive I will fail to thank someone who played an integral role in teaching me, encouraging me, or helping me in some way. Kindly forgive me and my aging brain...we're doing our very best. Please know that I'm so thankful to everyone who cheered me on along the way. You've been hearing about this book for a LONG TIME, and some of you are as excited as I am to finally hold a copy in your hands.

I'd like to specifically thank some super-special people who have walked with me the past few years and through the actual creation of this manuscript:

The readers of *God Speaks Today* (2008-2012) and *The Scoop on Balance* (2012-present): You read my words and offered encouragement and insight as I wrestled through all these concepts of hearing God's voice for the last 12 years. Because of you, I believed this would be a book someday. And now it is.

The listeners of *The Balanced MomCast*: Your excitement about the podcast fuels me to create more. I can't wait to see where this thing goes.

Rebekah F. and Julie C.: Thank you for enthusiastically agreeing to be early readers of the manuscript. Your comments, questions, suggestions, and encouragement helped shape this study in every possible way.

Mary Kathryn: Thank you for "voxing" me through the entire book-writing process. Your excitement about my book (and about the podcast while I was writing the book) got me over some of the biggest challenges of wrestling with this content. Thank you for brainstorming with me from beginning to end, being an early reader, and allowing me to bounce every idea off you. I can't believe we have never actually met in person, because I consider yours to be one of my most cherished friendships. Since I'm obviously not moving to Austin, please note our real-life coffee date has been relocated to Florida.

Ana, my OLBFF and editor: Thank you again for your keen eye, your insightful—and often hilarious—interjections, and for helping me re-word sentences that start with "there is." I love you.

To Jessica, Ruth, Denise, Shani, Ayisha, Mikki, Rose, Sarah, and Kelly: When I think of life-giving, life-speaking women, I think of you. Thank you for coming into my home, curling up on my couch and on my back porch, and covering me in prayer. You helped me fight a very real spiritual battle while writing this study, and I'm eternally grateful.

Mikki, Shani, and Ayisha: You challenge and inspire me to be a better student of God's word. I love our friendship.

Ruthoehler, Denise, Jessica, Valerie, Jennie, Julie, Mary K., Shani, and Rose: Thanks for the last-minute final read-through. You are the actual best.

The Women of New Life Church: What a fun three years we had. Of all the things I've ever done, serving as your Women's Ministry Leader goes down as one of my all-time favorites. I told you about this book the very first time I spoke to you. I'm so sad I won't be launching it with you (stupid COVID) or teaching it to you in person. I hope every time you think of me, you'll remember to Abide in Christ. "I am the vine, you are the branches; he who abides in Me and I in him, he bears much fruit, for apart from Me you can do nothing." John 15:5

Tim: Thank you for hearing God's voice and for interrupting that church service in July 2004 to quote Psalm 121 to the crying visitor-chick on the back row. I grew exponentially in the 16 years I sat under your leadership. Thank you for seeing the gifts in me and allowing me the distinct privilege of using them in every possible way at New Life Church. Also, thanks for being such a great friend—as I told you the week before I moved, you are the pastor I didn't know I needed. If you and Marlene ever want to start a church in Jacksonville, the Coopers are here for it.

Jennie: Thank you for being my BFF and the co-host of our fake radio program, *The Morning Show* (and also, *The Afternoon Show, The Evening Show,* and *The Morning Show: Weekend Edition*). Your friendship was (and is still) an answer to prayer. You remind me that all the hard things are LMTs. I'm sorry I moved. I miss your face. Please come to the beach.

Rebekah, Elijah, and Elliana: I love you so freaking much. Thank you for cheering me on in everything I do and for being genuinely proud of me. You really stepped up and showed maturity and responsibility when I slipped into the Writing Cave to complete this project in the weirdest year on record in the history of our lives. I couldn't be more proud of who you are. What an honor it is to be your momma.

Jon: Thank you for encouraging me to pursue the things I feel God is telling me to do and for trusting me when I say "I think God said…" I don't remember life before you and can't imagine life without you. I'm so excited that "Jacksonville called" and that we get to run the last leg of this race by the ocean…together.

Jesus: I don't have words to express how humbled and honored I am that You speak to me. Thank you for entrusting me with the words of Life. No matter how many photos I take of the ocean with my iPhone, I never come close to capturing the beauty I'm witnessing in real life while standing at the shoreline. That's exactly how I feel about this book. Please accept it as my feeble attempt at trying to describe the magnitude of what it means to walk and talk with You.

About the Author

Sandy Cooper is a Bible study teacher, podcaster, and writer. She helps frazzled women find peace.

She has been blogging since 2008 at **thescooponbalance.com,** and podcasts weekly at **The Balanced MomCast,** an award-winning podcast for overwhelmed moms. You can sometimes find her on *Facebook* and *Instagram* **@thescooponbalance**...but mostly, not. She recently moved back to Jacksonville, Florida with her family so she could live by the ocean forever.

Also by
Sandy Cooper

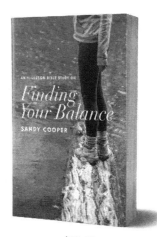

An 11-Lesson Bible Study on

Finding Your Balance

$14.99
Available on Amazon.com

Are you feeling overwhelmed?
Frazzled? Exhausted?

Do the items on your to-do list out number the hours in your day? Do you struggle to balance your priorities with the countless obligations and expectations vying for your time?

Does the idea of life-balance seem so far-fetched that you're starting to think it's nothing but a big fat lie?

Maybe you're thinking about balance all wrong.

It's time to release your unrealistic images of balance and embrace your actual, messy, beautiful life.

In *Finding Your Balance* you'll discover

- What God considers your highest priority so you can filter out things that don't matter.
- How to identify your strengths and weaknesses so you can determine the best ways to spend your time.
- How to overcome the Barriers to Balance—Comparison, Perfectionism, People Pleasing, and Busyness—so you can navigate life confidently, without distraction.

You will gain the clarity and focus to do the right things at the right time, so you can find the real balance you've been seeking.

Features:

- 11 in-depth Bible lessons to work at your own pace
- Workbook format, perfect for personal use or group study/discussion
- Practical applications and action steps
- Questions for reflection and discussion
- Scripture-based, lesson-specific prayers
- Humorous anecdotes (because Bible study should be fun!)